THE ILLUSTRATED
ENCYCLOPEDIA
OF
KNOTS

THE ILLUSTRATED ENCYCLOPEDIA OF

KNOTS

Geoffrey Budworth

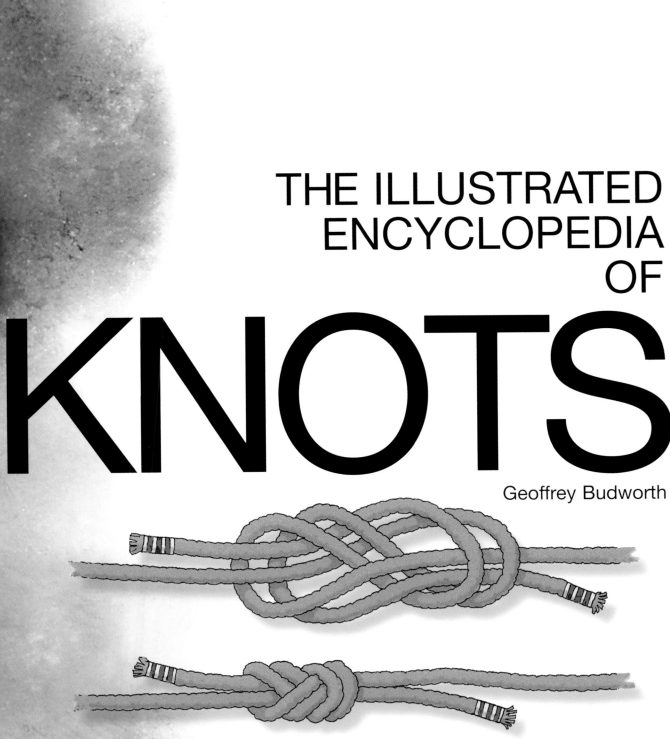

THE LYONS PRESS
Guilford, Connecticut
An imprint of The Globe Pequot Press

The Illustrated Encyclopedia of Knots

First published as a hardback edition 2000
First Lyons Press softback edition 2002

Original text and design © 2000 Thalamus Publishing

The Lyons Press is an imprint of The Globe Pequot Press.

Printed in China

ISBN: 1-58574-626-6

Illustrations: Oliver Frey
Knots photography: Steven Paul Associates
Project editor: Neil Williams
Design and Four-color work: Thalamus Studios

Note: While all reasonable care has been taken in the publication of this book, the publisher takes no responsibility for the use of the methods or products described in the book.

Picture Acknowledgments
Picture Research by Image Select International Limited.

All photographs copyright © 2000 Thalamus Publishing, except—
by kind courtesy of Marlow Ropes Limited: pages 10–11;
Allsport-Hulton Getty/Steve Powell: page 19;
Allsport-Hulton Getty: pages 20, 21
Gamma: page 9

CONTENTS

6   Introduction
7   A knotting history

10 GETTING STARTED
    Cordage materials
    Cordage construction
    Care of cordage
    Knotting terms
    Knot names
    Knot security
21 Tying tips

22 KNOT FINDER

23 SECTION 1—OVERHAND KNOTS
24 Simple overhand knot
25 Overhand knot with draw-loop
26 Angler's loop
28 Simple noose
29 Ashley's stopper knot
30 Overhand loop
31 Bag, sack or miller's knot
32 Tricorn loop
34 Fisherman's knot
36 Hunter's (or rigger's) bend
38 Zeppelin bend (Rosendahl's knot)
40 Reef (or square) knot
41 Wrapped and reef-knotted coil
42 West Country whipping
44 Water (or tape) knot
45 Round turn and two half-hitches
46 Fisherman's bend
47 Double overhand knot
48 Strangle knot
49 Strangle knot coil
50 Double overhand noose
51 Double fisherman's knot
52 Double overhand loop

53 SECTION 2—FIGURE OF EIGHT KNOTS
54 Figure of eight knot
55 Figure of eight knot (with draw-loop)
56 Figure of eight noose
57 Figure of eight hitch
58 Figure of eight loop
59 Figure of eight becket hitch
60 Sliding figure of eight bend
62 Figure of eight bend
64 Figure of eight twin loops
66 Figure of eight triple loops
68 Figure of eight coil

69 SECTION 3—BOWLINES & SHEET BENDS
70 Common bowline
72 Twin bowline bend

73 Water bowline
74 Double bowline
75 Bowline in the bight
76 Triple bowline
78 Eskimo bowline
80 Sheet bend (and with draw-loop)
82 Double sheet bend
83 One-way sheet bend
84 Three-way sheet bend

85 SECTION 4—CROSSING KNOTS
86 Clove hitch
88 Buntline hitch
90 Rolling hitch
92 Midshipman's hitch
94 Constrictor knot (and with draw-loop)
96 Double constrictor knot
98 Transom knot
99 Groundline hitch coil
100 Snuggle hitch
102 Double figure of eight hitch
104 Boom hitch

105 SECTION 5—OTHER USEFUL KNOTS
106 Common whipping
108 Timber and Killick hitches
109 Alpine butterfly knot
110 Reef (or square) knot loop
112 The frustrator
114 Highwayman's hitch
116 Pile, post or stake hitch
118 Pedigree cow hitch
120 Bull hitch
122 Prusik knot
124 Asher's bottle sling
126 Jug, jar or bottle sling
128 Braid knot
130 Square knot
132 Chinese cloverleaf
134 Matthew Walker knot
136 Chinese lanyard knot
138 Vice versa
140 Lapp knot
142 Carrick bend
144 Turk's head (3L x 4B)
146 Knife lanyard knot
148 Ring hitch
149 Turk's head (3L x 5B)
150 Turk's head (5L x 4B)
152 Turk's head (T-shaped)

156 Summary
157 Glossary of terms
158 Suppliers
159 Index

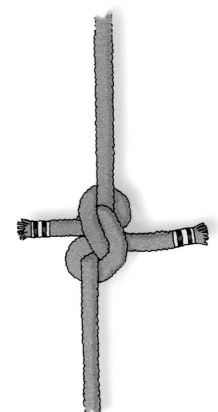

Introduction

It is a pleasurable craft and everyone can learn a few simple basic knots.

(John Hensel—*The Book of Ornamental Knots,* 198

Almost anyone, irrespective of age, gender and ethnic background, can learn to tie knots. Those unable to do so at present have simply not yet discovered that they can. They survive instead by means of adhesive tape, safety pins and superglues, elastic bands, clips and zippers, and other people's know-how. Which is a pity, because they are missing a lot of fun and satisfaction. Everyone ought to know a few knots. Anyway, there is a limit to how much hard-earned money should be spent on patented devices, which consume scarce planetary resources in their manufacture, when a length of rope or smaller cord and the right combination of knots work at least as well—often better.

In this book, learning one simple knot leads easily, by the addition of an extra turn or tuck, to mastery of more elaborate knots that are based on it, as the various bends, hitches, loops and stopper knots are cleverly grouped together according to appearance or layout and irrespective of function. Knots are more easily acquired in this way, their family relationships instantly apparent. For example, the bowline (a loop) is more closely related to the sheet bend (a joining knot) rather than to other dissimilar loop knots that may be only distant cousins. In the same way the tenacious constrictor (a binding knot) is just a tuck removed from the common clove hitch (an attachment).

The coming of beknottedness

It is not necessary to go boating to learn about knots. Indeed, most modern craft, with their factory-customized rigging and accessories, leave little scope for practical knot-tying. But there are still many aspects of work and leisure where performance is enhanced by the ability to tie the right knots: archery and angling; caving, climbing and conjuring; flying kites and fire-fighting; scuba diving and sail-boarding; tree surgery.

Weekend ramblers and wilderness pioneers, motorists and paramedics, all might find a use for a length of cord in their pockets. Even astronauts may need to tie a knot or two, in order to maneuver drifting hardware during extra-vehicular space walks, cord being a much

lighter payload than complex metal attachments. While many of us smitten by what the 19th-century scientist and mathematician Peter Guthrie Tait called "beknottedness" declare that tying knots is as pleasurable as doing a jig-saw puzzle, as satisfying as solving a crossword, and as delightful as reading an absorbing book.

For those who, like Tait (the man who also figured out how golf balls fly), prefer to apply the scientific method even to their pastimes, there is plenty to study where an original contribution may yet be made. Computerization of knots has barely begun. A comprehensive taxonomy (system of classification) has so far defeated exploratory attempts to map the theoretical interrelationships of the thousands of knots and their countless permutations. Then again, the practical ergonomics of exactly how and why knots work the way they do is still imperfectly understood. While knot theory, a purely mathematical approach (an abstruse kind of three-dimensional geometry), is a comparatively new but burgeoning field of research. "Knots cannot exist in four dimensions... However... they can be untied in four dimensions" teases Ronnie Brown, Professor of Mathematics at the University College of North Wales; and a Japanese research worker recently used laser beams as hi-tech tweezers to tie incredibly tiny knots in cut strands of DNA. Far from a dying art, knotting is a vigorous craft and science utilized by people of every class and creed. New knots are devised every year, but the knotting repertoire originated thousands of years ago.

Ancient Egyptians made long sea voyages—the most famous to the mysterious Land of Punt—thanks to their knowledge of ropes, binding, lashing and reefing knots.

A Knotting History

Cave dwellers tied knots, using them to snare and net food, to drag or lift loads—and to strangle enemies, tribal outcasts and sacrificial victims. The mummified bog bodies disinterred by archeologists in Northern Europe all have knotted ligatures around their necks. Knots pre-date written history. The unknown genius who first came up with a reef knot or a bowline must rank with those other individuals lost forever in the unreadable past who learned to control fire, harness the wind, cultivate the soil and make a wheel (all of which came after knotting).

Long before the Bronze, Iron and Stone ages there was an Age of Lashing, Snare and Thong, when humankind depended upon naturally occurring vines and plant fibers, augmented by the gut, sinews and rawhide lacings from the carcases of dead animals. All of those flint ax heads recovered by paleontologists once had bone or timber handles, which have long since decomposed and disappeared, together with the bindings that fixed one to the other. So, although some knots may be 100,000 years old, no evidence of their existence remains.

There is circumstantial evidence, however, from 20th-century tribes who lived a virtually Stone age existence, that early hominoids—who, while primitive, were certainly not simple—could have known the overhand knot and noose, as well as the granny and reef knots. The late Stone age lake-dwellers of Switzerland were useful ropemakers and weavers. One of the oldest knots yet discovered came from an archeological excavation of a submerged site under 10ft (3m) of seawater off the coast of Denmark, with the retrieval of a 10,000-year-old fish hook to which a short length of sinew or gut was still attached by means of the knot now known as a clove hitch. And in 1923, in Antrea (a pre-war region of Finland), a remnant of knotted fishing net was found preserved in a peat bog and scientifically dated at 7200 BC.

The ancient civilizations of Egypt, Greece and Rome, all employed expert ropemakers; but it is knots that make ropes work, justifying the considerable cost of their manufacture, and the Egyptians, Greeks and Romans all knew and tied quite complex knots for tasks as diverse as sailing boats, building projects, military campaigns, surgery and land surveying (a rope knotted into 12 equal parts can be pulled into a 3, 4, 5 right-angled triangle).

The Mycenaeans of ancient Greece, between 1600 and 1200 BC,

Roman army enginers of the late Republican period had developed sophisticated construction techniques for bridging rivers using timber at hand and ropes.

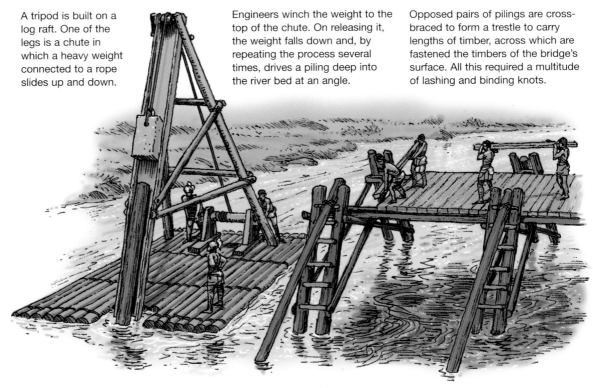

A tripod is built on a log raft. One of the legs is a chute in which a heavy weight connected to a rope slides up and down.

Engineers winch the weight to the top of the chute. On releasing it, the weight falls down and, by repeating the process several times, drives a piling deep into the river bed at an angle.

Opposed pairs of pilings are cross-braced to form a trestle to carry lengths of timber, across which are fastened the timbers of the bridge's surface. All this required a multitude of lashing and binding knots.

may have invented fly-fishing. Later, across the Mediterranean, the Egyptian Queen Cleopatra (c.68–30 BC) was reported to have been a keen and successful angler, who, it is fair to assume, tied her own fishing tackle. Knots tied in horse-hair, gut and silk for angling were later mentioned in the writings of British practitioners who included Dame Juliana Berners (or Barnes), the 15th-century Lady Prioress of Sopwell, and the later 17th century-gentlemen who included Gervase Markham, Robert Nobbs, Robert Venables and Izaak Walton.

Knotted cords have been used in many primitive cultures—from the Arctic to the South Pacific—to keep track of dates, events and genealogies; to recount folklore and legends (by means of the string figures known as cat's cradles); to serve as

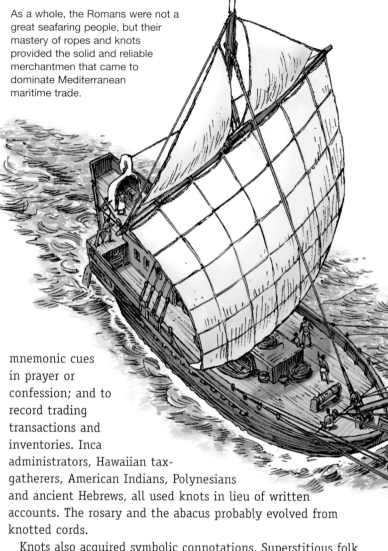

As a whole, the Romans were not a great seafaring people, but their mastery of ropes and knots provided the solid and reliable merchantmen that came to dominate Mediterranean maritime trade.

mnemonic cues in prayer or confession; and to record trading transactions and inventories. Inca administrators, Hawaiian tax-gatherers, American Indians, Polynesians and ancient Hebrews, all used knots in lieu of written accounts. The rosary and the abacus probably evolved from knotted cords.

Knots also acquired symbolic connotations. Superstitious folk believed they could cure (warts, for example) or kill. Charlatans were tried for bewitching the gullible by means of knot sorcery, and the Greek philosopher Plato (c.428–347 BC)—in his *Laws*—decreed death as the proper penalty for such a crime.

The growth of maritime knots

The medieval Venetians maintained a firm maritime grasp upon their widespread empire with a naval fleet, rigged from a massive ropewalk building, through the open-mouthed architectural gargoyles of which newly made rope spewed directly into the hands of the dockside riggers. There is, of course, an undeniably strong association between boats and ships and knots. Once crude dug-out canoes and rafts had grown too big and heavy to haul from the water between trips afloat, some kind of anchor or mooring line was needed. The earliest sailing ship required stays and shrouds to brace and support its single mast, with extra ropes to raise and trim its crude square-sail.

This standing and running rigging became ever more complex and sophisticated as voyages grew more venturous. From lake and river, to estuary, sea and ocean, knots evolved in versatility to match the demands made upon them. Deep-sea fisherman or merchantman, coastal smuggler or pursuing revenue officer, all who went afloat for whatever reason, had to know the ropes (literally) and the knots to tie in them. By the 18th century, the masts and spars of a lumbering 74-gun warship or a thoroughbred racing China tea clipper, strained under as much as 30 miles (48 kilometers) of rope rigging that weighed several tons. But this epoch of commercial and naval sail—now regarded with a nostalgia that (quite wrongly) assumes every able seaman had fingers like marlinespikes and hair like rope yarns—lasted barely 150 years. For every knot tied aboard ship throughout the last millennium, another was tied ashore.

Knotted ropes enabled miners to probe the deepest caves in search of fuel and ores deep underground; traders and explorers to trek on foot and with pack animals over and through desert, mountain range and jungle, in search of trade and treasure. Knotted cordage bucketed water up from wells and created the blocks-and-tackles with which stone masons built pyramids and ziggurats, castles and cathedrals. With knots British longbows were victoriously strung against whosoever was deemed to be the enemy at the time; church bells could be rung in alarm or celebration; kites might be flown; washing hung out to dry. While surgeons refined their suturing techniques, circus performers thrilled audiences with ever more daring feats on trapeze and tight-rope.

Bookbinders, cobblers, millers, butchers and shopkeepers of every kind, all employed a knot or two peculiar to their callings. So did farmers and falconers and steeplejacks. Weavers, their seemingly ramshackle looms worked by judiciously placed knotted linkages, joined broken yarns with a weaver's knot. Artful poachers made their own nets, since to buy them might alert the local magistrate. A rabbit net a yard (1m) high could be a hundred times as long, but it had to be light and small enough to carry concealed when out prowling. So they used lightweight threads—even silk (for birds).

Cennino Cennini (born c.AD 1372) wrote: "To make the perfect [artist's] brush take the bristles from a white hog, then tie them onto a stick using a plowshare knot." Five hundred years later the British Army ordered that: "...the greatest pains should be taken by the instructors to see that their men can make each of the knots here described in all situations." (*Instruction in Military Engineering—Vol. I*, 1st January 1870).

Universal knots

Cowboys in the American Wild West braided rawhide leather strips into horse harness, lariats and whips, tying knots as complicated as any sailorman's Turk's head, and even plaited watch-chains from their horses' tail hairs. They had learned this handicraft from the vacqueros of South America, and leather braider Bruce Grant later mused in writing that to trace the global spread of Spanish knots might add a fresh perspective to the growth and evolution of Spanish civilization.

Some basic knots probably arose spontaneously wherever, in various populated regions of the world, curiosity impelled someone to pick up a length of cord to find out what could be done with it. "Many knots, especially the simplest varieties, seem to be nearly culturally universal," observed Donald P. Ryan and David H. Hansen (*A Study of Ancient Egyptian Cordage* in the British Museum, 1987). Knowledge of others must have spread via commercial exchange and military conquest.

A bookcase can be filled with the hundreds of different editions in English of knotting publications, only a fraction of which are currently still in print. Add to them all later revisions and reprints, also translations into other languages, and it would be necessary to fix up extra shelves. Despite all of these knot books, however, competent knot tyers remain a rare breed. R.M. Abraham observed (*Winter Nights Entertainments*, 1932): "It is extraordinary how little the average individual knows about the art of making even the simplest knots." And Logan Persall-Smith (1865-1946) wittily confirmed; "I might give up my life for my friend, but he had better not ask me to do up a parcel." (*The Penguin Dictionary of Modern Quotations*, 1971). This is odd because it is an easy enough art or craft to grasp.

By the 16th century, the rigging of ocean-going ships had become an art that would grow ever more complex. The port of Lisbon, an engraving by Theodore de Bry.

Getting Started

No tool of any kind is needed to learn and then try out the knots in this book. All that is required is a couple of lengths of round, soft, flexible cord or thin rope, each around 6ft (2m) long, preferably differentiated by shade or hue, and no more than 0.39in (1cm) in diameter. Suitable cordage can be bought from many hardware stores, most camping and outdoor pursuits specialists, boat and yacht chandlers. Wholesalers may be listed under *Rope, Cord & Twine*, and from them you can generally receive details of a nearby retail outlet for their products.

CORDAGE MATERIALS

What little any knot tyer needs to know about cordage can generally be elicited from a reputable supplier. Those who plan to use knots in potentially hazardous activities, from hang-gliding to scuba diving, may wish to delve deeper into chemical composition, performance criteria and test data, all of which are obtainable from the publications of manufacturers' technical and sales departments. For the average user, a general knowledge of the main types of cordage construction, and the characteristics of the commonly encountered materials is all that is necessary to buy shrewdly and economically.

Natural (vegetable) fiber

All rope and other cordage was once made from the fibers of plants which were soaked, shredded, combed and graded prior to processing into yarns, strands and rope. Flax and jute came from plant stems; abaca (known as hemp) was obtained from leaves; cotton strands grew on seeds; with other natural sources as diverse as coir (from fibrous coconut shells) and esparto grass. Hunter-gatherers 100,000 years ago grew just one crop—flax for ropemaking. Fibers of animal origin came from horse, camel (and even human) hair, also wool and silk. Some of these products can still be obtained, at a premium price that reflects their subordinate share of today's cordage market.

These vegetable or natural fiber ropes emerged in colors from blonde to brown, with smells evocative of their plant sources and exotic countries of origin. Some nostalgic souls—who in their hearts wish humankind had not progressed beyond canals, windmills and sailing ships—still yearn for tarred Italian hemp (once the best cordage in the world), Philippine manila (from the leaves of a type of banana), sisal from the Yucatán peninsula of Central America, coir from the Malabar coast and Ceylon, and Egyptian cotton (seen in ropes aboard rich owner's yachts, or tied around the waists of nuns and monks).

Since the fibers obtainable from vegetable sources were limited in length from around 10in (23cm) to 3ft (1m) at most, natural ropes were always weak, even when scaled up to enormous circumferences. Nonetheless the countless fibers projecting from the surface of all natural cordage created the friction which enabled even quite basic knots, bends and hitches to hold in such ropes—but these hairy ropes could be cruel on the hands.

Such cordage swelled when wet, jamming the knots tied in them. In icy conditions, when wet ropes froze, any movement caused the brittle fibers to break and irreparably weakened affected strands. Vegetable fiber ropes had to be painstakingly dried before they could be stowed away, otherwise they were prone to mildew and rot, while insects and vermin might chew and destroy them at any time. Following the Second World War, when synthetic fibers came onto the cordage market, these shortcomings could no longer be tolerated.

Synthetic (manmade) fibers

Cordage of all kinds is nowadays made from artificial fibers of polyamide, polyester, polyethylene and polypropylene. These are the four manmade products that have emerged from chemical laboratories in the past 50 years, to be adopted by the cordage industry. They now dominate the market.

Polyamide (also known as nylon) is the strongest (although 10–15% weaker when wet). The first of the synthetic fibers to become commercially available for rope making, it was at the outset an expensive alternative that only a few customers could afford. There are two grades, nylon 6,6 (discovered in the Du Pont laboratories) and nylon 6 (subsequently developed by I.G. Farbenindustrie), the numbers indicative of their respective molecular structures. The main advantage of nylon ropes is that they stretch under load, by anything from 10–40%, regaining their original length when the load is removed. This makes them the obvious choice for tow-lines, mooring lines and any other use—such as climbing—where the energy of a sudden fall or other abrupt shock loading may have to be safely absorbed.

Polyester (sold as Terylene™ or Dacron™) came next, a British development resulting from research at the Calico Printers Association, the sole rights of which were taken up by Imperial Chemical Industries. It is about 75% as strong as nylon, but equally so wet or dry. It does not stretch half as much, and pre-stretching during manufacture can eliminate most of what latent elasticity it does possess. Consequently it is ideal for any sort of task, such as to replace wire stays or guy-lines, where high tensile strength must be coupled with an absence of noticeable stretch.

Polyethylene (Polythene) appeared in the late 1950s, when the simple hydrocarbon ethylene was incorporated into a rope making fiber. It was a cheaper product than either nylon or

Terylene, hard-wearing and durable; and, although the ropes made from it were not as strong as the other two, it was still superior to the traditional vegetable fiber yarns. With a density less than that of water, polyethylene was the first synthetic fiber to float. Practical enough for use in the fishing industry and for agricultural baling twines, it is less suitable for general-purpose knot tying.

Polypropylene represented the major break-through in synthetic fibers, however, when it was discovered that it could be polymerized (made into long molecular chains) to create a fiber considerably stronger and even lighter than polyethylene and extruded from low-cost machines. The raw material (a by-product of the oil industry) was very cheap, so that synthetic ropes made from it could at last compete with sisal and even manila on almost equal terms. It soon became available in a variety of forms, ranging from filaments to split-films which could be twisted into yarns to make a variety of cordage. Polypropylene ranks below nylon and Terylene in terms of cost and performance, but it is the most versatile of the synthetic fibers, and large quantities are made and sold at reasonable prices for domestic, industrial and sporting applications not requiring an exceptional performance.

Miracle fibers

Kevlar™ is an organic polymer (used for bullet-proof vests), which was discovered by Du Pont in 1965 and is the lightest of today's state-of-the-art fibers. Weight-for-weight it is twice as strong as nylon, and has less stretch than Terylene or Dacron. Advertising copy-writers have been tempted to compare it favorably with the strands of a spider's web. It is not that good. When a fly hits and tangles with a spider's web, it is equivalent to one of humankind's fishing nets withstanding the collision of a jumbo jet. Even Kevlar cannot cope with such an impact. It is so brittle that merely bending and flexing its fibers causes them to cut through one another, and ropes often consist of a Kevlar core sheathed in a protective braid of polyester.

Dyneema™ from the Far East, and its US counterpart HMPE (High Modulus Polyethylene), is marketed as Spectra™ by Allied Chemicals who began making this super-lightweight polyethylene in 1986. It is more tolerant of flexing than Kevlar, which it looks set to supersede.

Vectran™, is another high performance cordage produce, a thermoplastic multifilament yarn spun from liquid crystal polymer with a complete absence of stretch and—unlike Kevlar—with the ability to bend around tight radii.

PBO (Poly(p-phenylene-2,6-bezobisoxazole)) is yet another of these remarkable fibers, up to 20% stronger than either Vectran or HMPE.

Summary

Both nylon and terylene rate highly in terms of handling, durability, resistance to abrasion, rot and mildew, or exposure to alkaline chemicals. Nylon is more easily damaged than Terylene by contact with acid and its life is rendered significantly shorter than that of terylene by photo-chemical degradation through exposure to the ultra-violet radiation from sunlight (so store in a shady place). Both can be put away wet or dry. Polythene and polypropylene float, making them obvious choices for lifelines, ski-lines and other buoyant roles.

All synthetic cordage melts if subjected to extreme heat, and its surface will glaze and harden (impairing its function) at friction-generated lesser temperatures. Nylon and Terylene have the highest melting points, at around 473–482°F (245–250°C), but that is not much higher than the flash-point for paper. Even a lighted match will do irreparable harm to them, so keep cordage away from barbecues and decorators' blow torches. Polypropylene melts at about 302°F (150°C), while polythene is most vulnerable of all at something like 262°F (128°C).

The so-called miracle fibers, with their phenomenal power-to-weight ratios, represent the cutting edge of the cordage industry's technology; and, for those who value high performance beyond mere money, their expense is justified. They are neither necessary nor desirable for the knots featured in this book.

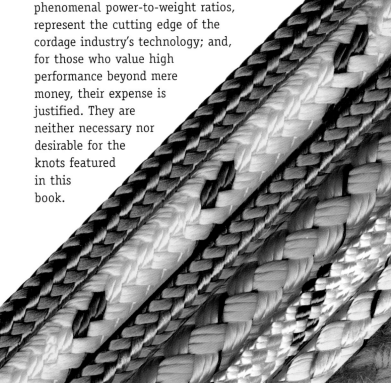

CORDAGE CONSTRUCTION

Strictly speaking the term rope only applies to cordage over 0.39 in (10 mm) in diameter. Anything less than this is referred to collectively as *small stuff*, which may be (in descending order of size) cord, spunyarn or twine. Small stuff of domestic quality is familiarly known as string or thread. Any rope with a particular function is a line (washing line, tow-line, guy-line, mooring line).

Ropemaking

The basic element of most synthetic cordage is a long extruded monofilament, which is a continuous fiber of uniform diameter and circular cross-section, larger than 50 microns (0.002 in). An alternative is the multifilament, which is a cluster of very fine synthetic fibers, each less than 50 microns. A batch of either mono or multifilaments is spun right-handed (clockwise) by machine to create a long yarn and a number of these right-handed yarns are next spun together in the opposite direction, left-handed or counter-clockwise, to create an individual strand. Finally a trio of these left-handed strands is then laid up right-handed (clockwise again) to make a traditional three-stranded or hawser-laid rope, known simply as a hawser (*figure 1*). It is all of this accumulated twist and counter-twist, imparted during manufacture, that causes the components of a rope to cling together and is responsible for its characteristic geometry, strength and flexibility. Right-handed rope is sometimes referred to as Z-laid and left-handed rope (a rarer commodity) as S-laid.

Catering to the nostalgic preference of some customers to handle hairy rope, cordage manufacturers all have at least one product that recaptures this quality in synthetic materials. They achieve this by deliberately chopping extruded filaments into short staple lengths, to roughly replicate natural fibers, and then spinning and laying them up in the usual way. Some of these ropes and cords, are even colored and given brushed matt finishes, to resemble hemp, jute, etc. They look the part in TV and film historical costume dramas, or as part of the decoration of a nautical theme bar, yacht club or restaurant. They may even be used, with care, to re-rig classic wooden ships, as long as the shortcomings of such cordage are borne in mind.

Plaited

For a rope of gigantic size—such as a mooring line for a supertanker—four pairs of large strands may be interwoven to end up as a plaited eight-strand cable (*figure 2*). This type of construction is not only flexible for crews to handle on deck, but it is comparatively easy to splice to an anchor chain.

Figure 1
The traditional three-stranded hawser-laid rope.
Below: a three-stranded rope of synthetic fiber
and, bottom, the same made from vegetable
material.

Fibers

Yarns

Strand

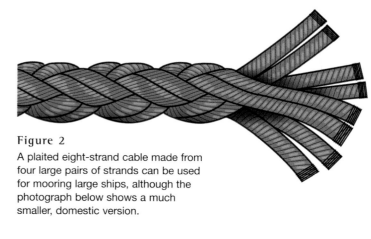

Figure 2
A plaited eight-strand cable made from
four large pairs of strands can be used
for mooring large ships, although the
photograph below shows a much
smaller, domestic version.

Braided lines

Only when the use demanded it (for flag halyards, sash cords in windows, ship's log-lines) was vegetable cordage braided.

In contrast, most synthetic cordage products are braided as opposed to laid (in strands). Braided ropes consist of an outer sheath of either 8 or 16 interwoven batches of yarns enclosing a number of core or heart yarns. These core yarns may simply run parallel through the middle of the rope (*figure 3*), or be hawser-laid (*figure 4*), or plaited (*figure 5*). This robust and versatile construction is known as sheath-&-core ("kernmantel" in some climbing publications) or braid-on-braid. There are even ropes with three layers, an outer sheath that encloses an inner sheath which surrounds the core (*figure 6*).

Braided lines not only combine strength and flexibility but incorporate other desirable features. For example, it is possible to have a nylon heart (for resilience) with an extensible Terylene sheath (to resist abrasion); or a Terylene heart of unyielding toughness, with a fluffy matt polypropylene outer sheath for comfortable handling.

All cordage—braided or laid—that is tightly tensioned during the manufacturing process is referred to as hard-laid. It will be durable but somewhat stiff (at least when new).

Figure 3
Parallel core braid rope and photographic example below.

Figure 4
Hawser-laid core braid rope.

Figure 5
Plaited core braid rope and, in the picture above, (right).

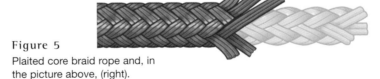

Figure 6
Three-layered core braid rope and, in the picture above, (left).

A reduced tension during manufacture results in a more flexible line that is said to be soft-laid.

Cordage never came cheap, Ropemaking used to be a labor-intensive craft, dependant upon the importation of raw materials from distant lands subject to fluctuations in trade brought about by uncertain global conditions (including wars). Frugal users bought their rope second-hand (or stolen) and, when eventually it was too old for further work, it would be

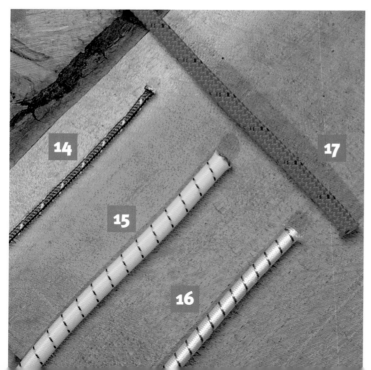

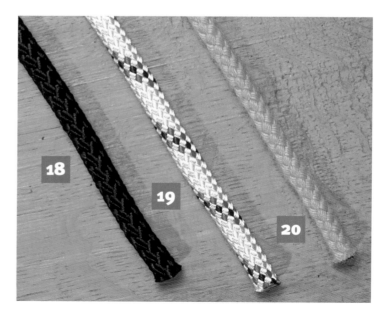

sold yet again—from which comes the expression "money for old rope"—to be picked apart and used as wadding (known as *oakum*) to caulk the seams and planks of wooden ships. It was a punishing task often given to prisoners. A disgraced Oscar Wilde, locked up in Reading gaol, wrote in 1898:

We tore the tarry rope to shreds
With blunt and bleeding nails.

Today, despite economies of scale achieved through reduced labor forces and increased mechanization, higher technical specifications mean that cordage remains a costly item.

Cost & color

Early manmade ropes were most often white, with maybe a single colored yarn spun the length of a rope to indicate its maker and so differentiate the product from those of a competitor. The British naval dockyards and many River Thames lighterage firms also required more elaborate colored combinations of what were known as rogue's yarns to deter theft of costly cordage.

In the latest ropemakers' brochures, the customer is dazzled by an artist's palette of primary colors, pastel shades and color combinations. It is now feasible to tie up garden plants with green string; to have blue lifelines for life-belts beside the swimming pool or boating lake; to tie disco dancing shoes with fluorescent pink laces; and for motor mechanics to reeve

Left: a selection of commonly available cordage
1. $^{9}/_{16}$ in (14 mm) blue monofilament polypropylene
2. $^{9}/_{16}$ in (14 mm) white nylon hawser
3. $^{9}/_{16}$ in (14 mm) buff-colored polyester
4. $^{1}/_{2}$ in (12 mm) white staple-spun (hairy) polypropylene
5. $^{1}/_{2}$ in (12 mm) white pre-stretched polyester
6. $^{5}/_{16}$ in (8 mm) green matt finish polyester
7. $^{1}/_{4}$ in (7 mm) orange polyethylene
8. $^{9}/_{16}$ in (14 mm) plaited white nylon anchor rope
9. $^{9}/_{16}$ in (14 mm) white (blue flecked) 16-plait braid-on-braid polyester
10. $^{3}/_{8}$ in (10 mm) in white (blue flecked) 16-plait matt polyester
11. $^{1}/_{2}$ in (13 mm) in blue (yellow flecked) 16-plait, sheath-sheath-core
12. $^{7}/_{16}$ in (11 mm) white (with fluorescent lime and black flecks) 16-plait sheath-&-core Spectra/Dyneema
13. $^{5}/_{16}$ in (8 mm), 8-plait extensible polyester sheath with nylon core
14. $^{1}/_{8}$ in (3 mm) sheath-&-core Spectra
15. $^{5}/_{16}$ in (8 mm) yellow sheath-&-core shock elastic (bungee) cord
16. $^{1}/_{4}$ in (7 mm) silver sheath-&-core shock elastic (bungee) cord
17. $^{5}/_{16}$ in (8 mm), 16-plait sheath-&-core Spectra/Dyneema
18. $^{3}/_{8}$ in (10 mm) black 8-plait multifilament polypropylene
19. $^{3}/_{8}$ in (10 mm), 16-plait sheath-&-core polyester
20. $^{3}/_{8}$ in (9 mm), 8-plait orange matt sheath-&-core polyester

their automobile engine hoists with black rope (so as not to show oily hand prints). The crews of ocean racing yachts, and even some dinghy sailors, are now accustomed to have color-coded halyards and sheets aboard their craft for quick identification, and a competitive edge to their boat-handling.

Rope's ends

Whatever the type and construction of rope, never cut it without first ensuring that the severed ends are prevented from first unraveling and then fraying. Synthetic hawsers in particular, lacking the cohesive friction of vegetable fiber ropes, will fall apart quickly; and a frayed end is impossible to work with, as well as being a costly waste of material.

Temporarily tie or tape either side of the place where the cut will be made. Use a pair of strangle or constrictor knots (*figure 7; pages 48, 94–95*), or a single piece of friction tape (*figure 8*), which can be sliced through the middle to secure both ends at a stroke. Alternatively, with synthetics, use a heated knife blade to sever and at the same time heat-seal the cut ends. There are even proprietary brands of "liquid whipping" (quick-drying, latex-based or polyvinyl acetate [PVA] glues) into which already cut and tied or taped ropes' ends can be dipped and then left to congeal and dry in the air.

Figure 7

Figure 8

Plastic tubing can be obtained from chandlers which, cut into short sleeves, is fitted over a rope's end and then heated (for example, by holding it over a steaming spout) to shrink and form an artificial whipping. Any one of these is merely a first aid measure although, if the old timers could have used them, I have no doubt they would have done so. But sooner rather than later the accepted semi-permanent treatment is then to apply a whipping, which is a neat and tight binding of spunyarn (for large hawsers) or twine (for smaller stuff), which are sold in balls and reels respectively. Use natural fiber on vegetable fiber cordage and synthetic on synthetic.

Care of cordage

It is only sensible to care for expensive cordage. Minimize fair wear and tear. Avoid carelessly dragging rope over rough ground or treading it underfoot. Protect sections that bear against sharp or abrasive fixtures or other hardware by enclosing them in tubing sleeves or wrapping them with tape or spunyarn. Vary predictable localized chafe by using a longer line than necessary, then shifting its position a little periodically. Alternatively, reverse it (end for end) from time to time. At least once a year wash ropes in water with a mild soap, or hose them down, to remove abrasive dirt and grit. Dry in fresh air and store them, hung up, away from direct sunlight.

In routinely handling ropes that are subjected to serious use, inspect them frequently to detect wear or damage. A slight fuzziness on the surface of a braided line is no cause for concern, and may even afford protection from further abrasion. Extensive areas of broken outer fibers are a warning sign, however, that the rope may have to be replaced. Open up the strands of hawser-laid ropes by gently counter-twisting them, to obtain a glimpse of the rope's inner condition. The state of a braided line's heart must remain unseen. Only gross flaws, such as a torn sheath through which some of the core protrudes like an organic rupture, or glazing due to heat-generated friction, will be apparent.

Signs of a sheath creeping over its core are symptomatic of greatly differing degrees of movement and implies that the construction is somehow failing. In the absence of a log book for a rope (which is seriously suggested for climbing ropes), only an intimate knowledge of what any braided rope has endured will determine when it ought to be downgraded from work where failure would be hazardous or costly to less crucial employment—like learning and tying knots.

Coiling

Rope and smaller cordage are perhaps the longest and thinnest artefacts made by humankind, and—in common with hosepipes and electric cables—they seem to have minds of their own. Even carefully stored ropes, when retrieved, are liable to tangle. Indeed, some knots—such as the overhand and the figure of eight—apparently tie themselves. There is only one way to ensure a reasonable chance of picking up a previously discarded rope and being able to put it to immediate use. It must be coiled.

Methods of securing a coil are described and illustrated elsewhere in this book. The golden rule, with laid line, is that right-handed rope must be coiled right-handed (clockwise), if it is to be kept tamed and ready for work. The reason for this is that, when a rope is uncoiled preparatory to use, any unwanted latent twist (present by the very nature of its construction) will tend to be absorbed by the strands opening up slightly. For this reason, left-handed rope—not often encountered—should be coiled counter-clockwise. Furthermore, as each turn of a clockwise coil is made, a subtle clockwise twist must also be inserted into the rope itself (roughly 360° of twist for each individual turn) to ensure that it lies flat.

Do the reverse with left-handed lines. Otherwise, at worst, a hard-laid rope will deform itself into a series of figures of eight; and, if that is allowed to happen, a real bird's nest of a tangle will result. In theory, deliberately coiling ropes in a succession of figures of eight would neutralize all possibility of unwanted torsion; but the reality is that such coils are awkward to make and handle; nor, in practice, are they necessary.

Braided rope may be coiled either clockwise or counter-clockwise but, so ingrained does the habit of coiling clockwise become, that most rope workers keep the faith and coil it clockwise too.

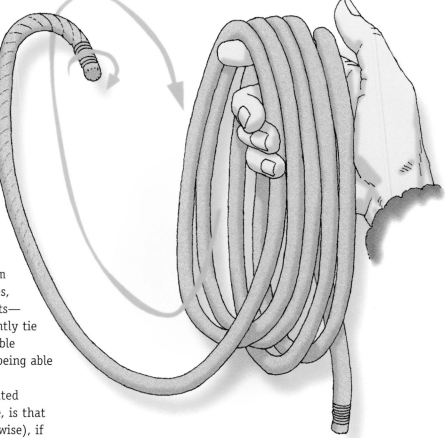

Knots Themselves

The established knotting repertoire consists of more than 4,000 specimens, and countless extra variations and permutations of these fundamental knots are possible; and yet many professionals and able amateurs, working afloat, or as fire-fighters, on civil engineering projects, as tree surgeons, or as a member of an assault-and-rescue team for hostage situations, admit to a sound knowledge of no more than six of those knots. More often than not these are: reef knot (*page 40*); sheet bend (*pages 80–81*); clove hitch (*pages 86–87*); round turn & two half-hitches (*page 45*); figure of eight (*pages 54–55*); and timber hitch (*page 108*). Now these—one binding knot, one bend, three hitches and a stopper knot—are fine, as far as they go, but not one is less than a thousand years old, and all evolved coping with vegetable cordage. In no other activity, I suggest, would such ancient (and perhaps outmoded) techniques go unquestioned.

The big problem with the 1950s synthetic cordage was that many tried and trusted knots no longer held securely in it. The new-fangled manmade ropes were smooth, slick and lacked frictional grip. Manufacturers' recommendations at the time, repeated by many knotting writers since, was simply to add extra turns and tucks. This led to some awkward and unattractive hybrid knots, when the more sensible solution would have been to look for others better suited to synthetic materials.

Some innovative knot tyers have in the last 20 years produced new knots for modern cordage (the vice versa bend is one), which have been adopted to become part of the established knotting repertoire. Others have resurrected and rehabilitated discarded or overlooked and underrated knots, such as the Eskimo bowline, which now prove admirably suited for manmade cordage. As the renowned knotsman Clifford Warren Ashley put it: "Old knots long out of use have a way of coming back into this workaday world with renewed usefulness."

Knotting terms

Individual knots can be grouped according to form and function. Those that join (bend) two ropes' ends together are called bends. Attaching a line to a ring, rail, spar, post, stanchion or other fixed anchorage point is done with a hitch. Handier than hitches, and often used instead of them, are fixed single, double or multiple loops, while sliding loops are known as nooses. To prevent a line pulling free from a block, fairlead, hole or slot in some hardware fixture or accessory, a stopper knot is used. Knots for packages, bandages, or to tie off the neck of sacks are binding knots. Groups less often used include shortenings.

In manipulating any rope or cord to tie a knot, and

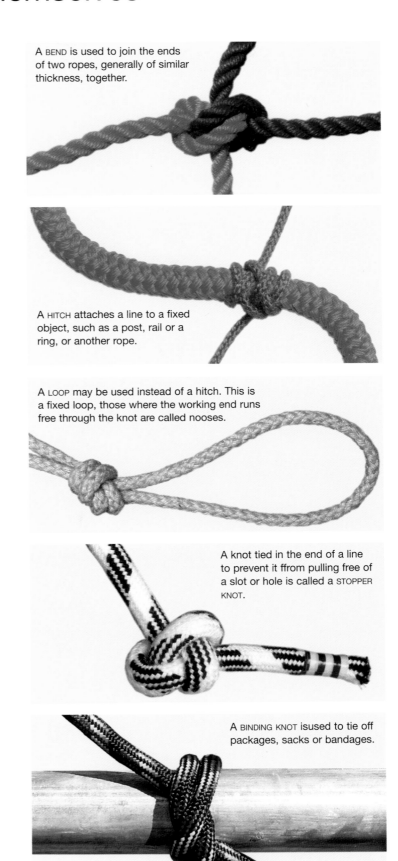

A BEND is used to join the ends of two ropes, generally of similar thickness, together.

A HITCH attaches a line to a fixed object, such as a post, rail or a ring, or another rope.

A LOOP may be used instead of a hitch. This is a fixed loop, those where the working end runs free through the knot are called nooses.

A knot tied in the end of a line to prevent it ffrom pulling free of a slot or hole is called a STOPPER KNOT.

A BINDING KNOT isused to tie off packages, sacks or bandages.

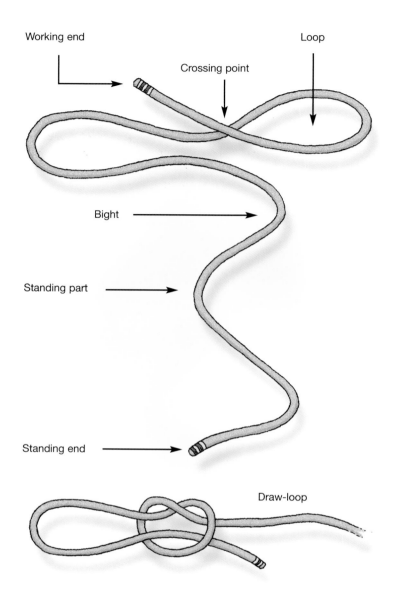

Working end

Loop

Crossing point

Bight

Standing part

Standing end

Draw-loop

Knot names

A few knots are nameless—and, since anything without a name is innominate, I call these orphans "innominknots"—but most have a name. Some are descriptive, such as the figure of eight knot (*pages 54–55*); some imply a person or place of origin, like Ashley's stopper knot (*pages 28–29*) or Alpine butterfly (*page 109*); others suggest the primary use or function, the angler's loop (*pages 26–27*) for example; and a few are enigmatic or whimsical, such as the vice versa (*pages 138–139*) and knute hitch.

Although most knots fall into discrete categories, their family relationships can be hard for an outsider to discern, while some maverick individual knots can be downright misleading. The fisherman's knot is mostly used as a bend; and, due to a semantic quirk by which sailors always spoke of "bending" a line to ring or spar, the fisherman's bend is actually a hitch. The reef knot has been called a flat knot, and is widely known in the USA as the square knot, which makes it necessary to find an American alternative (rustler's knot is one) for the other knot that the British call a square knot.

Several knots have more than one name. The double fisherman's knot (*page 51*) is called the grinner knot by anglers, and the weaver's knot is just another sheet bend. It was this muddled knotting nomenclature that caused Desmond Mandeville, a founder-member of the International Guild of Knot Tyers, to end a poem in which he exhorted inventive knot tyers to name their new knots with the wry conclusion:

But worse than those that have not any,
Some knots there be that have too many.

Knot strength

In the days of vegetable cordage, when a rope broke under load it was often observed to do so close to the knot and it was deduced that knots somehow weakened the lines in which they were tied. For instance, the simple overhand knot (*page 24*) reduces the breaking strength of an unknotted rope by more than a half, and the practice arose of calling it 45% efficient, so the breaking strength of a rope with an overhand knot tied in it is only 45% of that claimed by the manufacturer for the new unknotted line. The reef knot (*page 40*) is almost as weak.

Knots with gentler curves and less severe nips proved less destructive. The clove hitch (*pages 86–87*) and the round turn & two half-hitches (*page 45*) are at least 70% efficient, that is, they reduce the breaking strength of any rope in which they

especially when describing the process to another knot tyer, the active end of the line is referred to as the **working end**. The opposite and inert end is the **standing end** and everything in between is the **standing part**. Any section of line that is bent into a U-shape is a **bight**. Where one rope part overlaps another a **crossing point** occurs; and, when a bight incurs a crossing point, it becomes a **loop**. When the working end is not pulled completely through the knot, a **draw-loop** is formed, which, when tugged, acts as a quick-release device to untie the knot. The double reef bow (used to tie shoe laces) has twin draw-loops, while the highwayman's hitch (*pages 114–115*) is entirely made up of one draw-loop after another. Many other knots may be usefully modified with a draw-loop. That part of a knot where the friction is concentrated is known as the **nip**.

Right: When you are hanging from a vertical cliff face, it is not only the breaking strength of the rope that matters, but also the strength and the security of the knots you tie in the rope.

are tied by no more than 30%—but still a considerable percentage. Clearly, when ropes were likely to be operating close to their breaking strengths, the choice of the strongest knots was a serious consideration and a matter for shrewd and experienced judgment.

Modern synthetic ropes and cords are often so immensely strong, however, that knot strength is a less significant factor than it used to be. Indeed, it is a common practice (and it is one that must delight rope sellers) to buy much thicker lines than are strictly necessary for the job envisaged, because the one that could actually cope would be too thin to grasp comfortably by hand. Even so, where it is considered useful to be aware that a knot is significantly stronger or weaker than another, the fact will be mentioned.

Knot security
Some knots that are considered fairly strong under a steady load, such as the bowline (*pages 70–71*), may be decidedly less dependable when subjected to intermittent jerking or shaking. In other words, they are insecure. Security of knots is a separate consideration from knot strength. Smooth, slippery

and slimy materials, as well as any that are likely to shake or be pulled in all directions by wind, wave or rough usage, require secure knots.

As some knots featured in this book are both strong and secure, why use any other? The simplest knot for the purpose should always be preferred. Knots may have to be tied in difficult conditions, in the dark, when hands are numb, or body and brain exhausted, and then simple and familiar knots may be all that will work. Often, too, a knot is tied by one person but then untied—perhaps to be cast off in a few life-saving seconds—by someone else. For these reasons, it tends to be the simplest and commonest knots, bends and hitches, a compromise blend of strength and security, that are preferred by cautious knot tyers. Of course, there are occasions when only a more complicated knot will do. Then use it.

Knots are like tools. One might go a lifetime using, misusing and abusing a saw, a hammer and a screwdriver; but craftsmen and women collect as many different ones as they can, so as to be able to put their hands on precisely what they need when they need it. And knots—unlike tools—cost next to nothing to acquire, and (as they are carried around in one's head) weigh nothing and need no large toolbox to hold them.

The law of loop, hitch & bight
Slide or lift a clove hitch off its post or other foundation and, bereft of its attachment, it falls apart and ceases to exist. A number of hitches can be undone this way. Some loop knots also collapse and vanish if a single crucial retaining bight is removed. All of the knots that can be untied in this way, without withdrawing an end, share a common yet curious property. They can be tied in the bight, that is, without recourse to a working end.

Tying knots in the bight is a rapid, almost sleight-of-hand, technique that is always worthwhile—and is sometimes indispensable. In summary, if a knot can be untied in the bight, it can be tied in the bight. This previously unsuspected natural law was identified by retired research scientist Dr. Harry Asher, a founder-member of the International Guild of Knot Tyers, who first published it in *A New System of Knotting —Volume 2* (1986) and later in *The Alternative Knot Book* (1989). Self-evident—like many brilliant insights—only after it has been pointed out, does this rule enable knot tyers to look for quicker ways to tie some knots (and to know when not to bother). For instance, the strangle and constrictor knots are physically similar in most respects, but the constrictor can be tied in the bight and the strangle knot cannot.

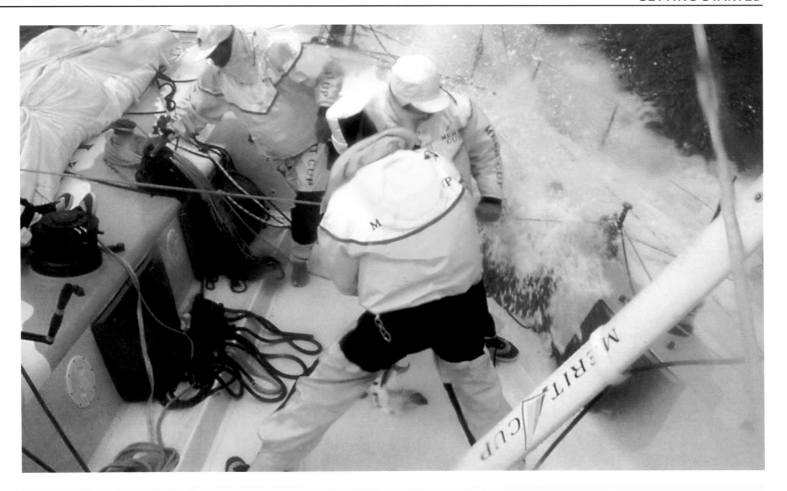

TYING TIPS

● A knot is either right, or completely wrong. One tuck amiss or astray and an entirely different knot—or no knot at all—results. And closely related knots may be very different characters; for example, just one tuck away from the sheet bend lurks the unbalanced thief knot (a reef knot, except that the two ends emerge on opposite sides) that, like Robert Louis Stevenson's Dr. Jeckyll and Mr. Hyde, exists in two forms, one stable, the other highly unstable.

● A knot is only as effective as the cordage in which it is tied. Elastic shock (bungee) cords shed previously reliable old stand-bys, such as the bowline, but will hold in others (like the angler's loop and the vice versa). It is a matter of finding the right knot for not only the job but the material being used.

● Very few knots (the reef knot is one) can be tightened by merely pulling on both ends. Others must be coaxed and kneaded into shape, then carefully tightened a bit at a time to eliminate slack (until no daylight is left between the various knot parts) and last of all by applying a tightening pull. Even then it is desirable to do so evenly, to each

working end and standing part in turn, however many there may be (the bowline in the bight has six). So, with any knot "work snug and then tighten."

● Learn to tie knots in the dark, since knotting in real life must often be done in such handicapped situations.

● For the same reason, untying knots can be an equal challenge; so train to identify them by touch, eyes shut, and dismantle them that way too.

● Practice does not always make perfect but practice does make permanent. Having learnt to tie any one of the knots in this book correctly, repeat it often so as to transfer it from short-term memory into long-term memory (an effective way to polish your own skills is to teach someone else how to tie a knot). Only then can any knot be left alone in the mind with a realistic expectation that it can be retrieved when needed next week, next year, or in 25 years time.

For a knot, once mastered, should last a lifetime. Knots forgotten were never truly learned in the first place. A good memory for knots is not a gift, it is a reward for curiosity, interest and active involvement during the learning stage. So let's get started. Knotting ventured, knotting gained.

Knot Finder

CATEGORY	SECTION	PAGE
Bindings		
Asher's bottle sling	Five	124
Bag, sack or miller's knot	One	31
Constrictor knot	Four	94
Constrictor knot (with draw-loop)	Four	95
Double constrictor knot	Four	96
Double figure of eight hitch	Four	102
The frustrator	Five	112
Jug, jar or bottle sling	Five	126
Reef (or square) knot	One	40
Strangle knot	One	48
Transom knot	Four	98
Turk's head (3 lead x 4 bight)	Five	144
Turk's head (3 lead x 5 bight)	Five	149
Turk's head (5 lead x 4 bight)	Five	150
Turk's head (T-shaped)	Five	152
Whipping, common	Five	106
Whipping, West Country	One	42
Lanyard knots		
Chinese cloverleaf	Five	132
Chinese lanyard knot	Five	136
Knife lanyard knot	Five	146
Matthew Walker knot	Five	134
Square knot	Five	130
Loops, fixed (single)		
Alpine butterfly knot	Five	109
Angler's loop	One	26
Bowline	Three	70
Double bowline	Three	74
Double overhand loop	One	52
Eskimo bowline	Three	78
Figure of eight loop	Two	58
Overhand loop	One	30
Reef (or square) knot loop	Five	110
Tricorn loop	One	32
Water bowline	Three	73
Loops, fixed (double, triple)		
Bowline in the bight	Three	75
Figure of eight triple loops	Two	66
Figure of eight twin loops	Two	64
Triple bowline	Three	76
Loops, adjustable, running, sliding		
Double overhand noose	One	50
Figure of eight noose	Two	56
Midshipman's hitch	Four	92
Simple noose	One	28

CATEGORY	SECTION	PAGE
Shortenings		
Braid knot	Five	128
Coil, figure of eight	Two	68
Coil, ground line hitch	Four	99
Coil, strangle knot	One	49
Coil, wrapped and reef-knotted	One	41
Stopper knots		
Ashley's stopper knot	One	29
Double overhand knot	One	47
Figure of eight knot	Two	54
Figure of eight knot (with draw-loop)	Two	55
Overhand knot	One	24
Overhand knot (with draw-loop)	One	25
Bends		
Carrick bend	Five	142
Double fisherman's knot	One	51
Double sheet bend	Three	82
Figure of eight becket hitch	Two	59
Figure of eight bend	Two	62
Fisherman's knot	One	34
Hunter's (or rigger's) bend	One	36
Lapp knot	Five	140
One-way sheet bend	Three	83
Sheet bend	Three	80
Sheet bend (with draw-loop)	Three	80
Sliding figure of eight bend	Two	60
Three-way sheet bend	Three	84
Twin bowline bend	Three	72
Vice versa	Five	138
Water (or tape) knot	One	44
Zeppelin bend (Rosendahl's knot)	One	38
Hitches		
Boom hitch	Four	104
Bull hitch	Five	120
Buntline hitch	Four	88
Clove hitch	Four	86
Clove hitch (with draw-loop)	Four	86
Figure of eight hitch	Two	57
Fisherman's bend	One	46
Highwayman's hitch	Five	114
Pedigree cow hitch	Five	118
Pile, post or stake hitch	Five	116
Prusik knot	Five	122
Ring hitch	Five	148
Rolling hitch	Four	90
Round turn and two half-hitches	One	45
Snuggle hitch	Four	100
Timber and killick hitches	Five	108

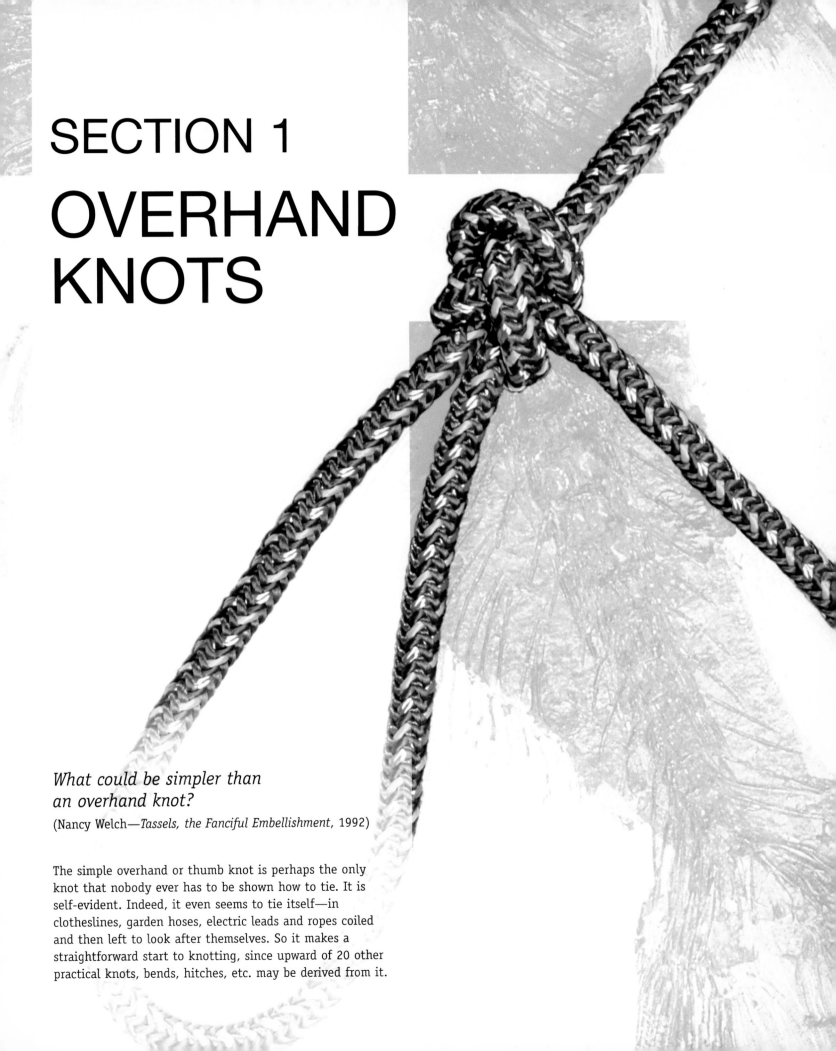

SECTION 1
OVERHAND KNOTS

*What could be simpler than
an overhand knot?*
(Nancy Welch—*Tassels, the Fanciful Embellishment*, 1992)

The simple overhand or thumb knot is perhaps the only
knot that nobody ever has to be shown how to tie. It is
self-evident. Indeed, it even seems to tie itself—in
clotheslines, garden hoses, electric leads and ropes coiled
and then left to look after themselves. So it makes a
straightforward start to knotting, since upward of 20 other
practical knots, bends, hitches, etc. may be derived from it.

SIMPLE OVERHAND KNOT

Purpose

This basic knot is used to stop any kind of line, from a cotton thread to a heavy-duty tow-rope, from pulling out of whatever work it is employed to do, whether that is assembling a block-and-tackle, attaching cord to a toddler's pull-along toy, or re-stringing a musical instrument. It can also act in a first aid capacity to prevent a line from fraying.

Tying

Simply make a loop, pull the working end through and then tighten the resulting knot (*figures 1–3*). Observe how the twin knot parts spiral to the right or clock-wise. All knots have a mirror image; in this instance, it is one in which the knot parts spiral to the left or counter-clockwise (*figures 4–6*). Tie whichever comes naturally. It is essential to recognize and be able to reproduce whichever is required, however, as some knots (such as the fisherman's knot) must only be tied with a pair of overhand knots of identical handedness. Others—like the reef knot (*page 40*)—need a couple of half-knots of opposite-handedness.

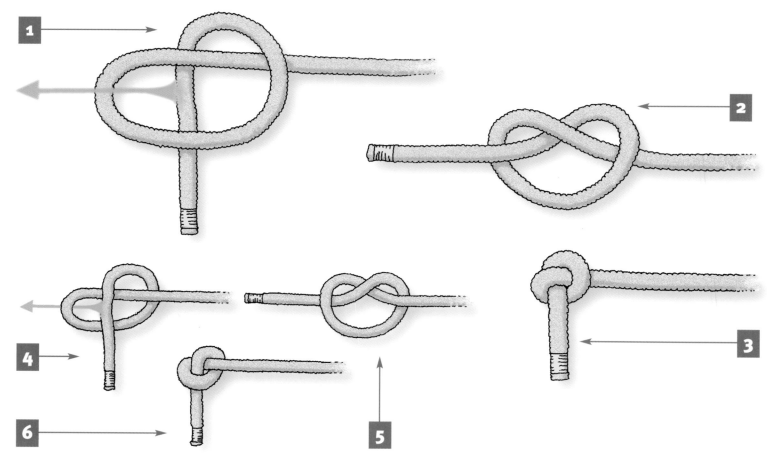

OVERHAND KNOT WITH DRAW-LOOP

Purpose

This knot is easier to untie than the basic overhand knot (which can be impossible to undo once it has been pulled tight).

Tying

Use a longer working end, which is not pulled entirely through the initial loop (*figure 1*). Then tighten the knot (*figure. 2*).

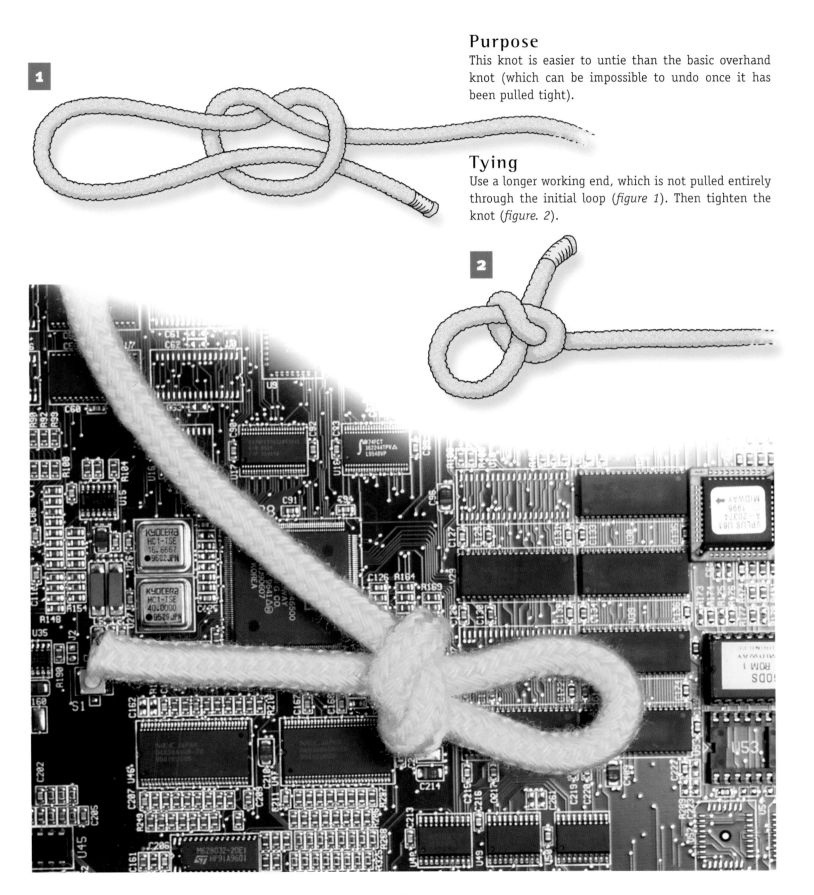

ANGLER'S LOOP

Purpose

Use this splendid knot to make a fixed loop that is secure in almost any material, even stretchy elastic shock (bungee) cord which escapes from many other knots.

Tying #1

Begin by loosely tying an overhand knot with a draw-loop (*figure 1*). Extend the loop to the required size and then wrap and tuck the working end as shown (*figure 2*). Work the resulting knot snug and tight by repeated gentle pulling on standing part, working end and both loop legs in turn, until the knot assumes its distinctive final form (*figures 3–4*).

Tying #2

Knowing what the completed knot looks like, there is a quick and smoother method of tying this loop knot in the bight (*figures 5–7*).

Knot lore

The angler's loop worked well in old-fashioned horsehair, gut and silken fishing lines, when it would be tied in a line or leader as the start for various tackle systems (hence its name), and it is believed by some to date back at least to the days of the 17th-century angling writer Izaak Walton.

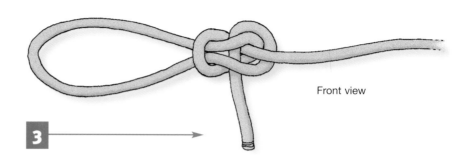

3 →

Front view

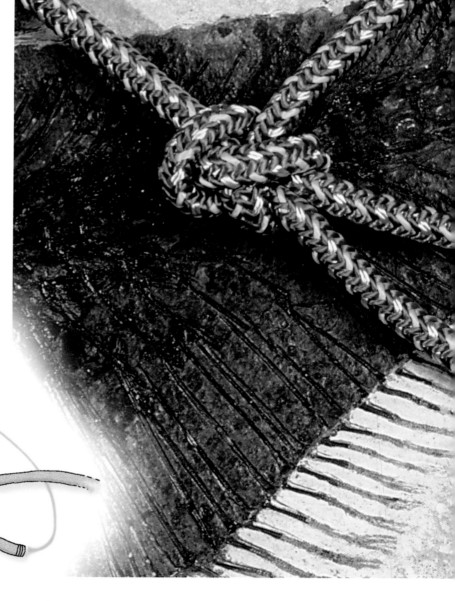

1 →

2 →

26

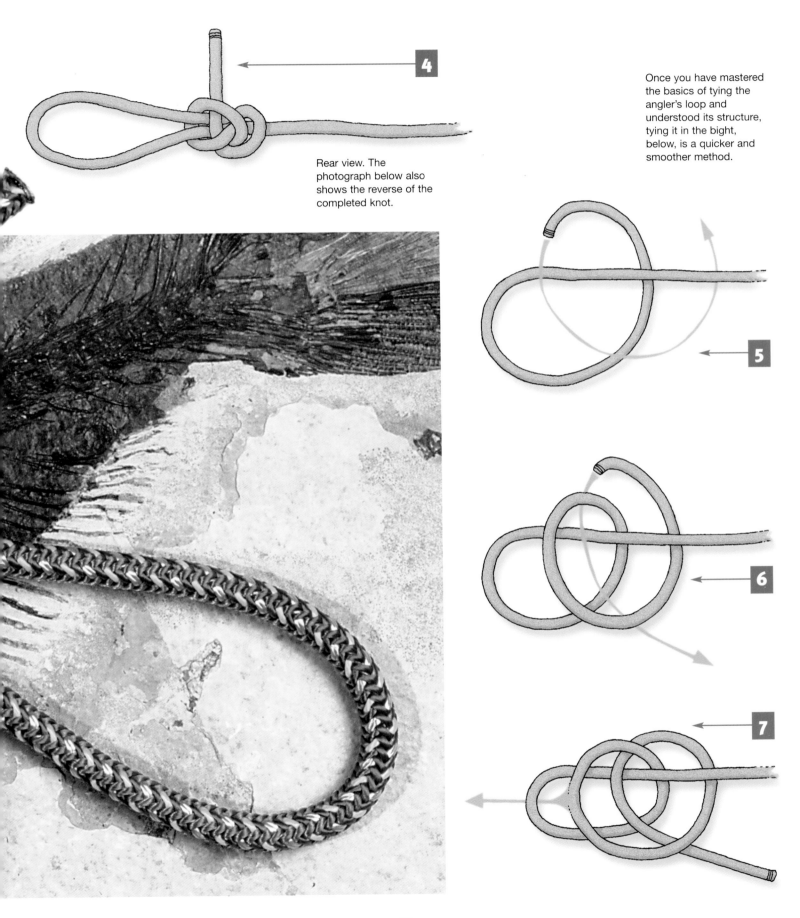

4

Rear view. The photograph below also shows the reverse of the completed knot.

Once you have mastered the basics of tying the angler's loop and understood its structure, tying it in the bight, below, is a quicker and smoother method.

5

6

7

27

SIMPLE NOOSE

Purpose
A simple sliding loop that tightens when pulled is handy for starting any sort of simple lashing, from a parcel to a luggage rack load.

Tying
Utilize the standing part of the line, and work away from the nearest end, to tie what would otherwise be an overhand knot with a draw-loop (*figures 1–3*).

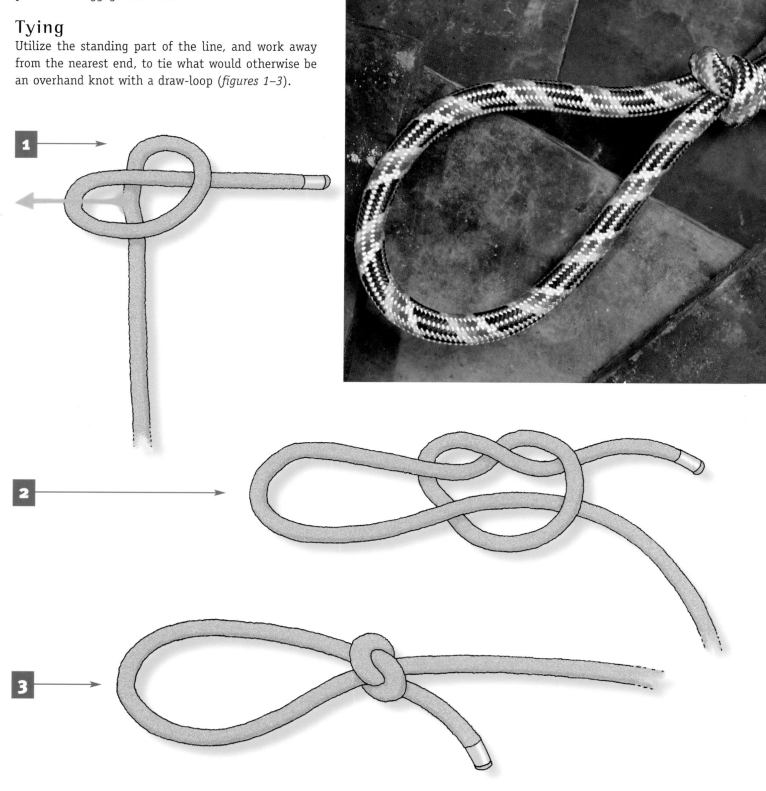

1

2

3

ASHLEY'S STOPPER KNOT

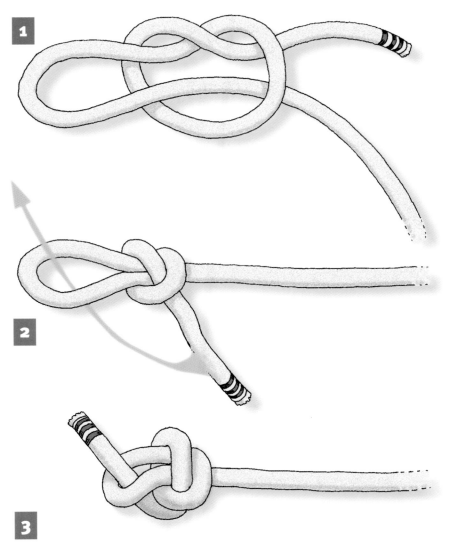

Purpose

This bulky knot will block a hole or slot out of which lesser knots pull free. The overhand knot and the figure of eight knot, for example, share a sort of hare-lip imperfection where they surround the standing part of the line in which they are tied. When a bigger stopper knot is needed, this is the one to use.

Tying

Tie a simple noose (*figure 1*). Tighten the running overhand knot, then tuck the working end as shown (*figure 2*). Finally pull on the standing part of the line, closing the loop to trap the end (*figure 3*). Note the neat tricorn arrangement, on the underside of this stopper knot, where it surrounds the standing part of the line. It is this feature that renders the knot more effective than most.

Knot lore

The artist and knotsman Clifford W. Ashley discovered this knot over 90 years ago when he was illustrating the cultured oyster industry for *Harper's* magazine. Spotting a bulky knot that he could not identify aboard one of the fishing fleet, this was his attempt to reproduce it. A few days later, when he had a chance to examine the mystery knot up close, it turned out to be nothing more than a wet, swollen and misshapen figure of eight knot. But this knot (the first of his numerous knotting discoveries), which he erroneously called the Oysterman's stopper knot, has survived as a minor classic in the established knotting repertoire.

OVERHAND LOOP

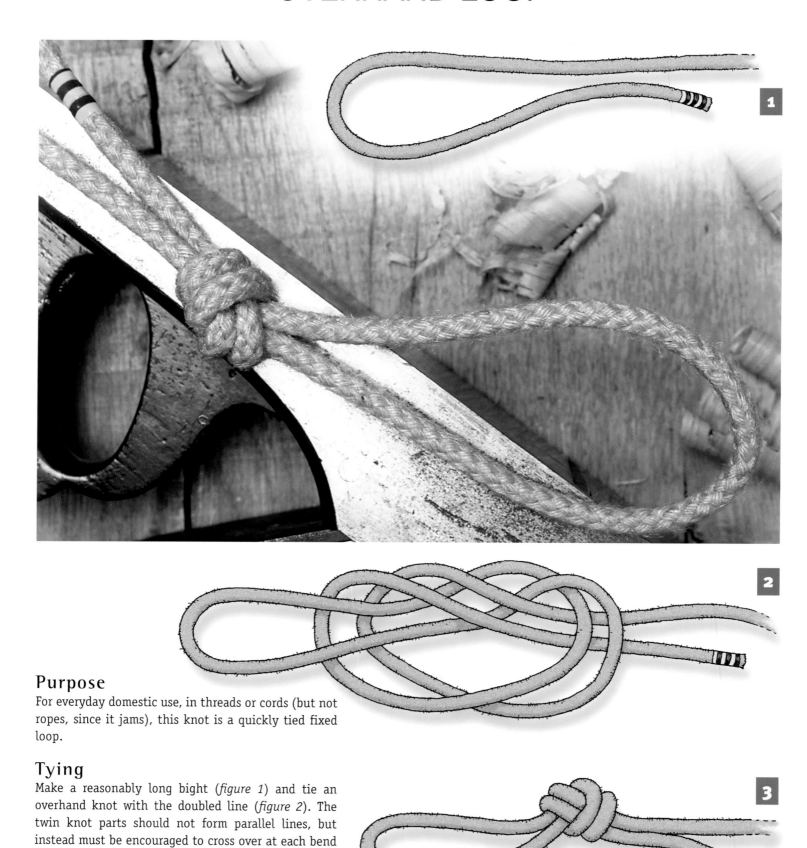

Purpose

For everyday domestic use, in threads or cords (but not ropes, since it jams), this knot is a quickly tied fixed loop.

Tying

Make a reasonably long bight (*figure 1*) and tie an overhand knot with the doubled line (*figure 2*). The twin knot parts should not form parallel lines, but instead must be encouraged to cross over at each bend so that, as it is tightened up, the knot beds down snugly (*figure 3*).

30

BAG, SACK OR MILLER'S KNOT

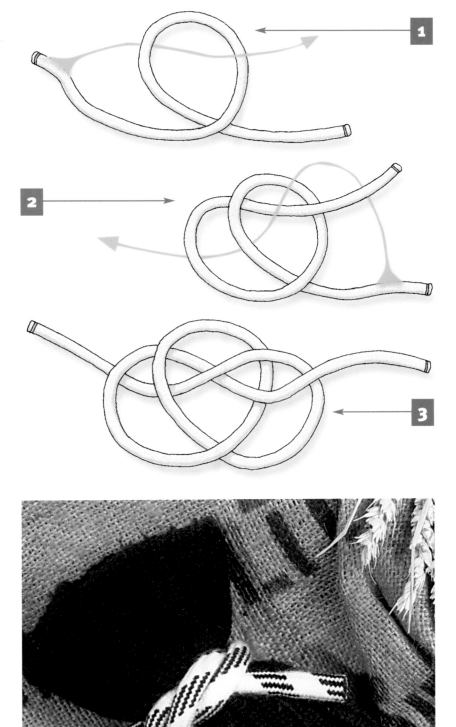

Purpose

To seize and close the neck of a bag or sack, use this binding knot which relies for its security upon being pressed against whatever it is tied around.

Tying

Make a loop and tie an overhand knot (*figure 1*). Tuck the other working end (*figures 2–3*) and arrange as shown (*figure 4*). Place the result around the bag or sack and pull on both ends to tighten into the final rope-like appearance (*figure 5*).

Knot lore

This is my own contrivance and will not be found in other knot books, although I doubt whether it is wholly original. Someone else can probably claim to have used it before me.

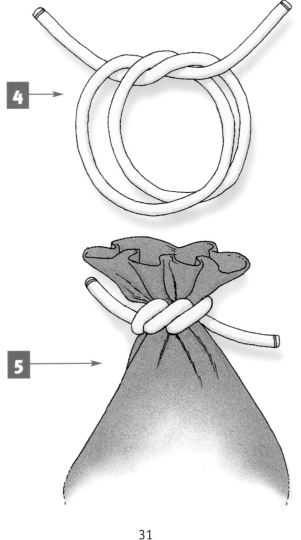

TRICORN LOOP

Purpose

This fixed loop is more secure than a common bowline. It also has a small amount of adjustment within it, enabling a washing line, a guy line or an archer's bow string to be tensioned or slackened as required. At first glance it resembles the Eskimo bowline (*pages 78–79*), and they could double for one another, but this knot has an extra crossing point.

Tying

Tie an overhand knot and then open the twin knot parts to create an imperfect figure of eight layout (*figure 1*). Tuck the working end over-under-over as shown (*figure 2*). To tighten this knot, pull on both the standing part of the line and the loop leg indicated (*figure 3*), when it will capsize into its final compact form (*figure 4*). The size of the loop can be reduced by first loosening the knot's nip around the sharp bight contained within it, and then pulling through a longer working end. Conversely, if a long working end was left when the knot was first tied, the loop may be lengthened by a similar process.

Knot lore

This is another of my own knots. I make no claim that it is original but, because of the neat three-cornered texture on both sides of this knot, I have named it accordingly.

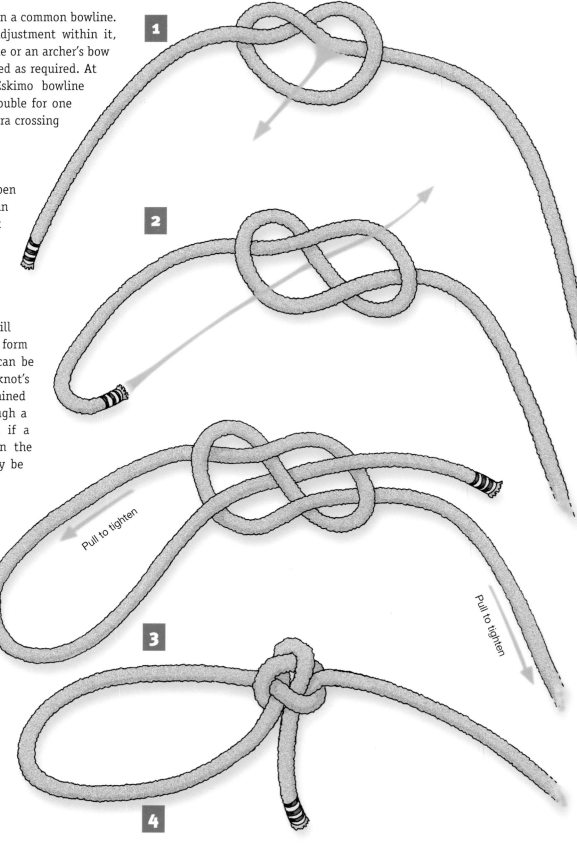

FISHERMAN'S KNOT

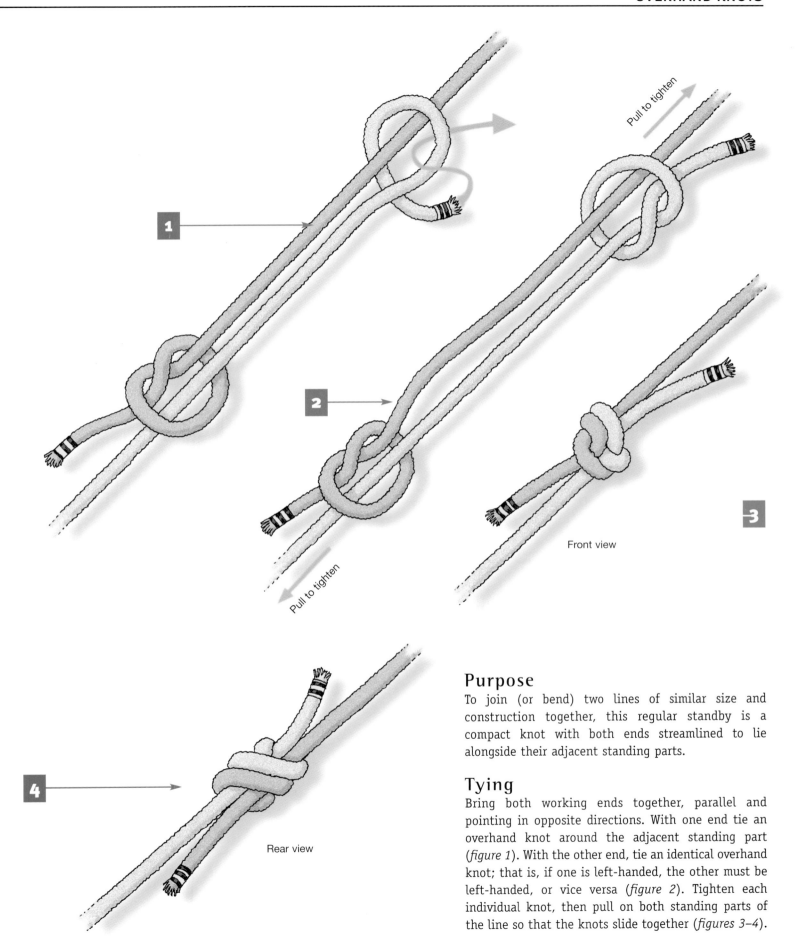

1

Pull to tighten

2

Pull to tighten

Front view

3

Rear view

4

Purpose

To join (or bend) two lines of similar size and construction together, this regular standby is a compact knot with both ends streamlined to lie alongside their adjacent standing parts.

Tying

Bring both working ends together, parallel and pointing in opposite directions. With one end tie an overhand knot around the adjacent standing part (*figure 1*). With the other end, tie an identical overhand knot; that is, if one is left-handed, the other must be left-handed, or vice versa (*figure 2*). Tighten each individual knot, then pull on both standing parts of the line so that the knots slide together (*figures 3–4*).

HUNTER'S or RIGGER'S BEND

Purpose

This mid-20th century knot joins two ropes or cords. It is strong and secure, but can be prised loose when the load has been removed.

Tying

Form two interlocked loops, as shown (*figure 1*) and then tuck each working end in turn to transform the initial layout into a couple of interwoven overhand knots (*figure 2*). Coax the knot into shape and tighten it. This is one of the best of an entire family of bends comprising two overhand knots, its recognizable hallmarks being the obliquely entwined couple of knot parts (*figure 3*) and a pair of twin bights (*figure 4*). By rolling these two bights down (into the page) the knot can be readily loosened and then untied.

The tying method illustrated is not Dr. Hunter's—which was prone to go wrong in unfamiliar hands—but one first described by that innovative knot tyer Dr. Harry Asher, a founder-member of the International Guild of Knot Tyers in *A New System of Knotting—Volume 1* (1986), and then published in *The Alternative Knot Book* (1989).

Knot lore

On Friday, 6th October 1978, the *Times* newspaper of London devoted a 28-cm (11-in) column on its front page to a report that retired consultant physician Dr. Edward Hunter had invented this new knot. Other newspapers ran the story, naming the knot Hunter's bend. I was contacted and between us we shared the load of radio and television interviews that followed.

Knot tyers around the world wrote to us for more information. Then—with all of this publicity at its height—the American physicist Amory Bloch Lovins tactfully pointed out to me that the knot had already appeared in an obscure 1950s US booklet called *Knots for Mountaineers* by Phil D. Smith, simply named as a Rigger's bend.

Smith had discovered the knot for himself in 1943 while working on the San Francisco waterfront. When contacted, he generously stated that Dr. Hunter was welcome to any publicity he attracted; and, as a consequence of the media attention, so many knotting enthusiasts came into contact with one another, that it became possible, in 1982, to establish the International Guild of Knot Tyers.

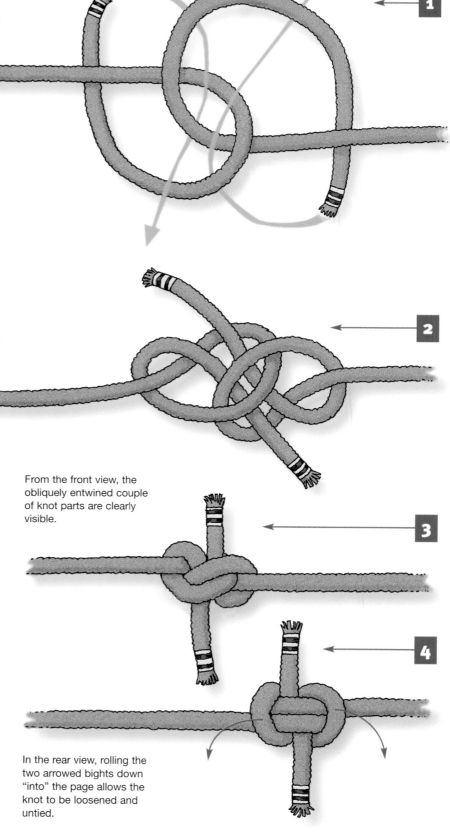

From the front view, the obliquely entwined couple of knot parts are clearly visible.

In the rear view, rolling the two arrowed bights down "into" the page allows the knot to be loosened and untied.

ZEPPELIN BEND (OR ROSENDAHL'S KNOT)

Purpose

Also known as Rosendahl's knot (see Knotlore below), this is a reliable heavy-duty alternative to Hunter's bend, and is preferable to it when the load is likely to be applied while the knot is still loose. Hunter's bend needs to be worked into shape before it is loaded, whereas this knot will pull up into a compact form of its own accord.

Tying #1

Some find this method of tying the bend easier. Hold both working ends parallel and together (*figure 1*). Tie a half-hitch in the nearest strand, so that it encloses the other one (*figure 2*). Now bring the standing part of that second strand forward, as shown (*figures 2–3*) and tuck its working end through the central compartment common to both cords (*figure 4*). The completed knot (*figure 5*) is symmetrical, with ends protruding from it at right-angles to the standing parts of both lines. This tying method was devised by Ettrick W. Thomson of Suffolk, England, to overcome the somewhat awkward way in which Rosendahl's knot was originally taught.

Tying #2

Form two loops and overlap them (*figure 6*), tucking the working ends to create a pair of interlocked overhand knots (*figure 7*). Tighten the knot (*figure 8*). This tying method was another of those first described by Dr. Harry Asher in *A New System of Knotting—Vol. 1* (1986) and then published in *The Alternative Knot Book* (1989).

Knot lore

US aeronaut hero, Lieutenant Commander Charles Rosendahl skippered the gigantic dirigible *Los Angeles* in the 1930s, and, according to marlinespike seamanship instructor Joe Collins, who served under him, he insisted that this knot should be used to bend his craft's bow mooring line to the fixed ground line. The knot was used by the US Navy for mooring its lighter-than-air ships until 1962.

The Zeppelin bend can be loaded even before it is completely tight (as in figure 4). To untie it, loosen the two bights and then undo the knot.

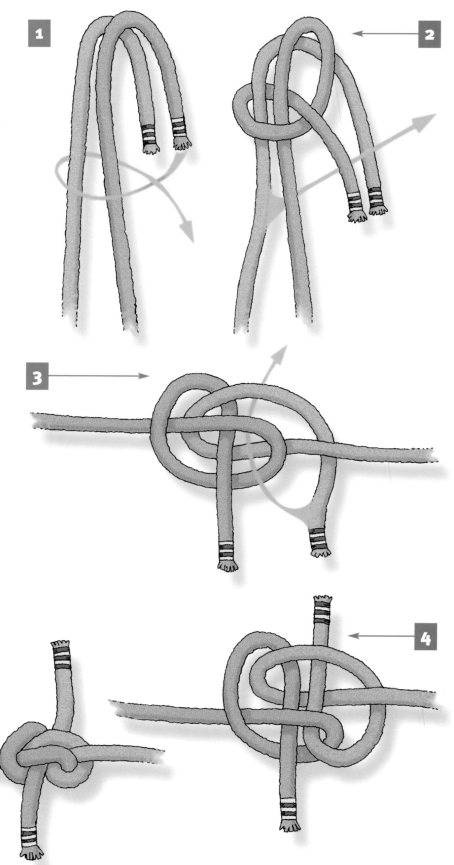

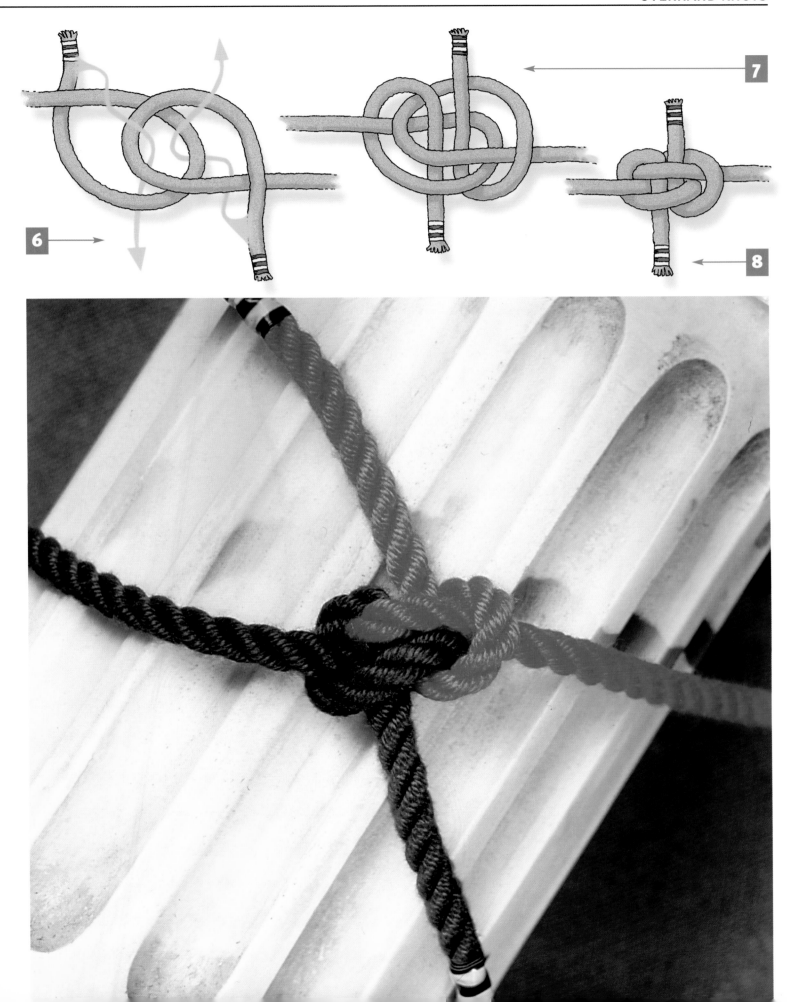

6

7

8

REEF (OR SQUARE) KNOT

Purpose

This is a binding knot for use in threads, string and other small cords. Use it only to fasten both ends of the same piece of small stuff, when it is strictly for bandages and packages, including the reefing of sails aboard dinghies and yachts that have traditional reefing points. With twin draw-loops it is the knot used to tie shoe laces (when it is called a double reef bow). It relies for its security upon bearing against whatever it is tied around, and is also a weak knot (reducing the breaking strength of whatever it is tied in by as much as a half). For these reasons it must never be used as a bend to join two working ropes.

Tying

When an overhand knot is tied in two ends of the same twine or cord around some foundation (or a space) it is known as a half-knot. Half-knots, like overhand knots, may be left-handed or right-handed depending upon the direction in which their knot parts helix. To make a reef knot, tie a single half-knot (*figure 1*), then add a second half-knot of opposite handedness (*figure 2*). In this example repeat the instruction: "Left over right, then right over left." The result is a flat knot, consisting of two interlocked bights, with both working ends emerging on the same side of the knot (*figure 3*).

Knot lore

Stone age cave dwellers almost certainly knew the reef knot. So did the ancient Egyptians, Greeks and Romans (who called it the Hercules knot), and distinguished it from the granny knot which, because it can both slip and jam, is less reliable. Incidentally, the granny knot is not thought to be a slur on the knot-tying ability of grandmothers, but is more likely to be a corruption of "granary knot" (from its use as a bag, sack or miller's knot). The Roman historian and scientist Pliny the Elder (AD 23–79) made an odd claim for the Hercules knot, writing in his *Natural History* that wounds bound with it healed quicker. Whatever his justification for this assertion may have been, first aid instructors today still insist that bandages and slings must be reef-knotted (although they are unaware of Pliny's reason for saying so). Emphasizing the unsuitability of a reef knot for use as a bend, the British craftsman and Master Mariner Stuart E. Grainger wrote in 1985:

Reefing a sail or tying a parcel,
A reef knot the role will fulfil.

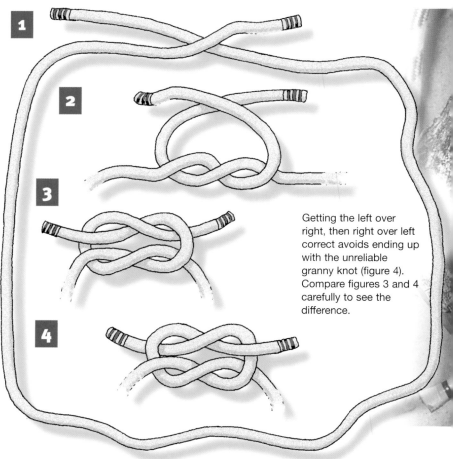

Getting the left over right, then right over left correct avoids ending up with the unreliable granny knot (figure 4). Compare figures 3 and 4 carefully to see the difference.

But joining two ends one should only use bends,
And a reef knot's a sure way to kill.

And in 1988 knot researcher Desmond Mandeville, added:

Eh, what grief for the poor wee Danny.
He intended a Reef but it turned out a Granny.

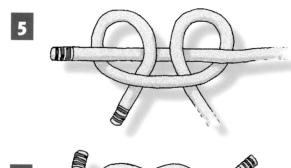

You can undo a reef knot by pulling on one working end and breaking the knot into a lark's head. It is then easy to slide one part off the other (figure 5).

For extra security, half-hitch each working end to its adjacent standing part (figure 6).

WRAPPED & REEF-KNOTTED COIL

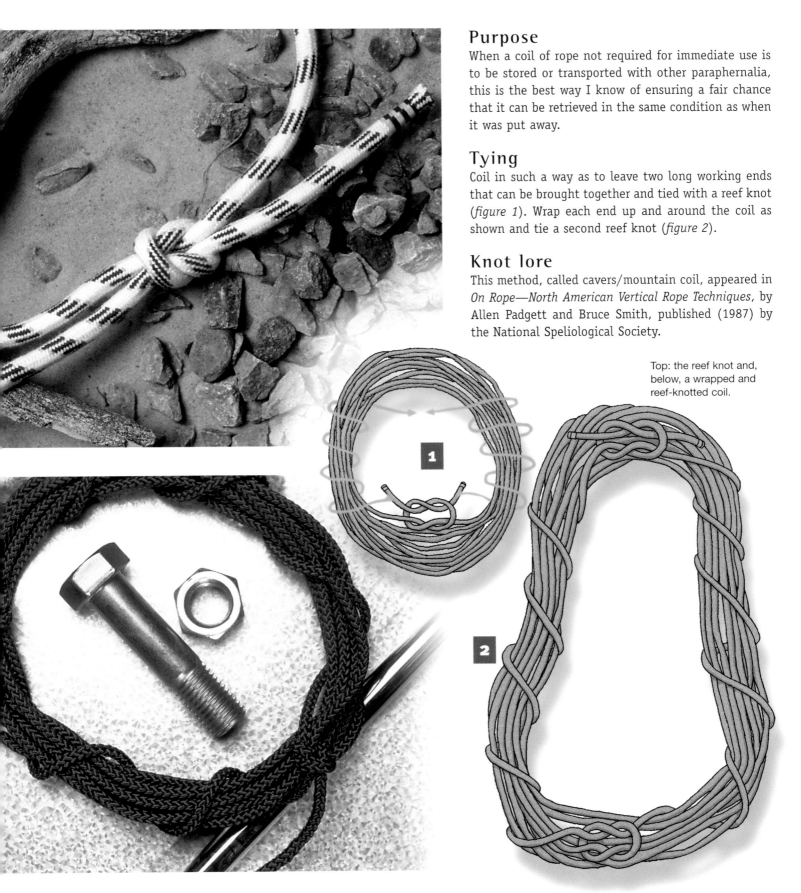

Purpose
When a coil of rope not required for immediate use is to be stored or transported with other paraphernalia, this is the best way I know of ensuring a fair chance that it can be retrieved in the same condition as when it was put away.

Tying
Coil in such a way as to leave two long working ends that can be brought together and tied with a reef knot (*figure 1*). Wrap each end up and around the coil as shown and tie a second reef knot (*figure 2*).

Knot lore
This method, called cavers/mountain coil, appeared in *On Rope—North American Vertical Rope Techniques*, by Allen Padgett and Bruce Smith, published (1987) by the National Speliological Society.

Top: the reef knot and, below, a wrapped and reef-knotted coil.

WEST COUNTRY WHIPPING

Purpose

A series of half-knots is a robust way to secure the cut end of a rope, especially a hawser-laid one, to prevent it from fraying. It rarely comes adrift as, even if ends come untied or one of the wrapping turns is accidentally severed by rough usage, the remainder of the whipping remains intact until it can be replaced.

Tying

Tie a half-knot around the rope at the site where the whipping is to start and pull it tight (*figure 1*). Turn the work over (or carry both ends around to the back) and tightly tie a second half-knot of identical handedness (*figure 2*). Return to the front and add a third similar knot (*figure 3*) and, turning the work over again, tie a fourth (*figure 4*).

Continue (*figure 5*) until a series of half-knots, snugly embedded alongside one another, has been constructed. Finish off with a reef knot (*figure 6*) and bury the ends, by either poking them beneath the whipping or stitching them into the rope with a stout needle. Note—for clarity this whipping is illustrated in thicker stuff than actual whipping twine which is strong but thin.

Knot lore

Some ropework devotees consider this whipping a botched job, assuming that whoever ties it knows no neater alternative. The fact is that it stays put when the quicker, but less secure, so-called sailor's method comes loose and falls off.

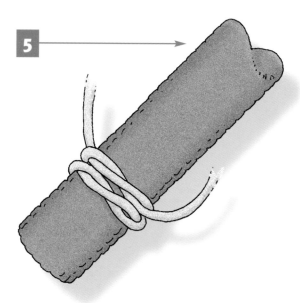

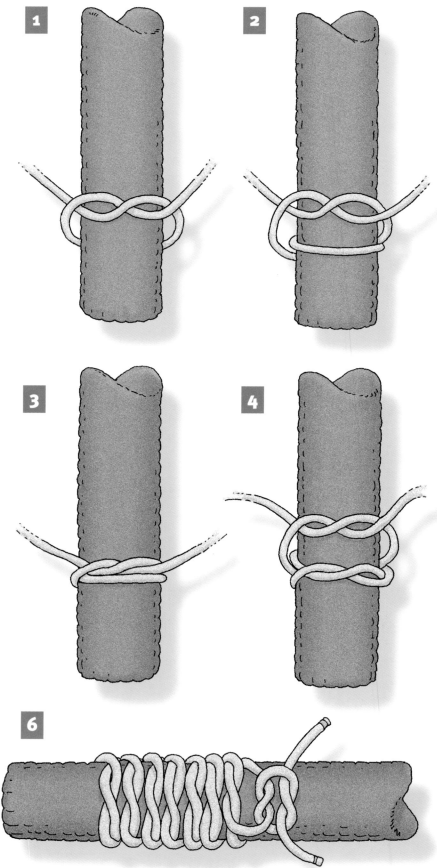

WATER or TAPE KNOT

Purpose

This knot is ideal for thinner cords, twines and monofilaments. It is also the only knot recommended by climbing authorities for use in flat tape (not illustrated). In ropes it tends to jam.

Tying

Start with a half knot, then tuck each working end as shown (*figures 1–2*). Encourage the knot parts to cross over at each end of the knot (avoiding parallel lines) and contrive it so that the two outer bights—marked "X" in the diagram (*figure 3*)—are in the standing parts of the line, since the knot is thought by some to be stronger that way. Finally pull it tight (*figure 4*).

Knot lore

This may be the "water knot" recommended for fishing lines by Dame Juliana Berners (Or Barnes), Prioress of Sopwell, in her *Treatyse of Fyshinge wyth an Angle* (published in 1496). If so, it pre-dates Izaak Walton's reference to the knot in *The Compleat Angler* (1653) by a century and a half.

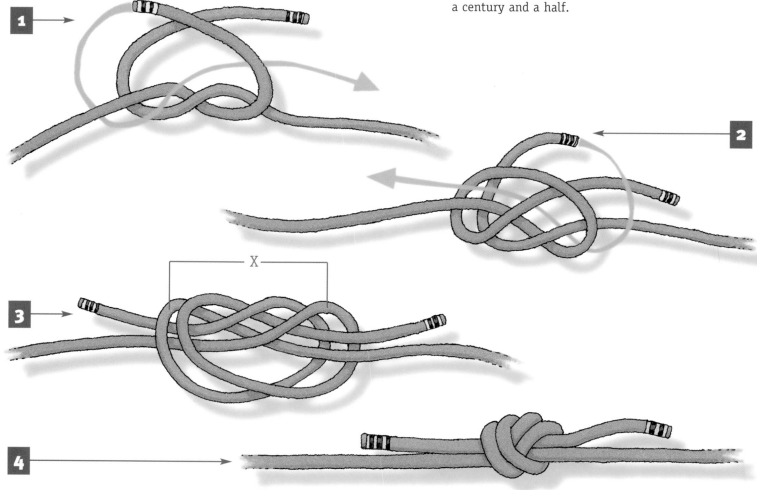

ROUND TURN & TWO HALF-HITCHES

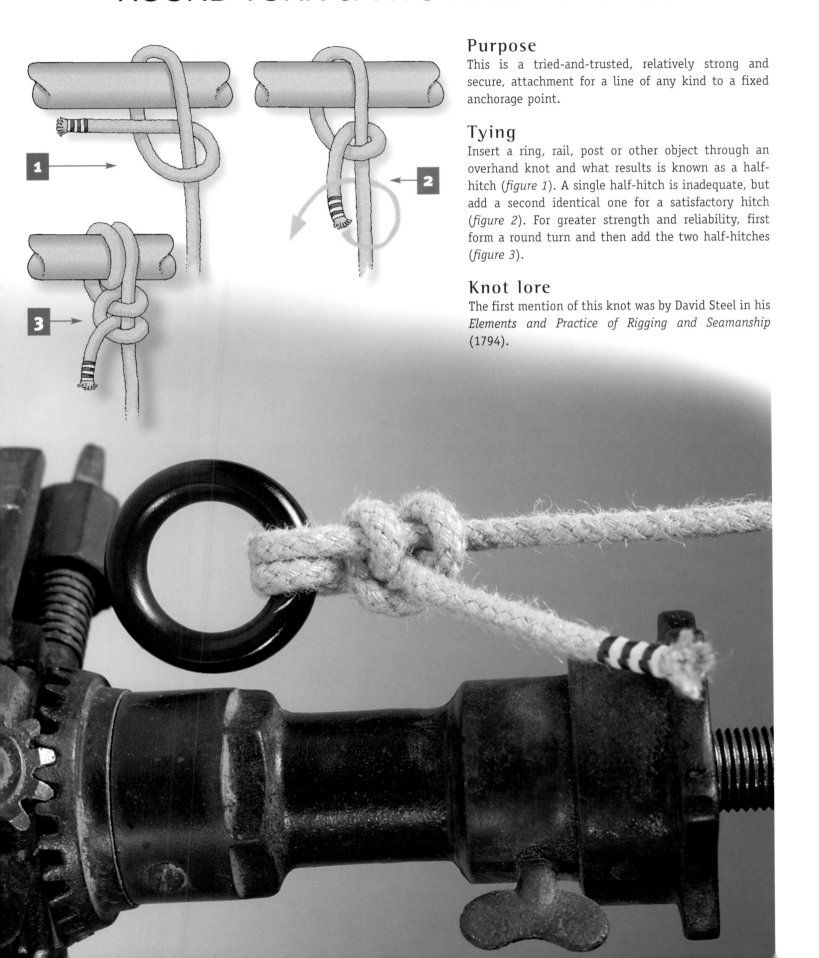

Purpose
This is a tried-and-trusted, relatively strong and secure, attachment for a line of any kind to a fixed anchorage point.

Tying
Insert a ring, rail, post or other object through an overhand knot and what results is known as a half-hitch (*figure 1*). A single half-hitch is inadequate, but add a second identical one for a satisfactory hitch (*figure 2*). For greater strength and reliability, first form a round turn and then add the two half-hitches (*figure 3*).

Knot lore
The first mention of this knot was by David Steel in his *Elements and Practice of Rigging and Seamanship* (1794).

FISHERMAN'S BEND

Purpose

Use this more secure variant of the round turn and two half-hitches in slick or slippery line.

Tying

Take a round turn and pass the working end through it to trap the first half-hitch (*figure 1*). Add the second half-hitch and tighten the whole knot (*figure 2*).

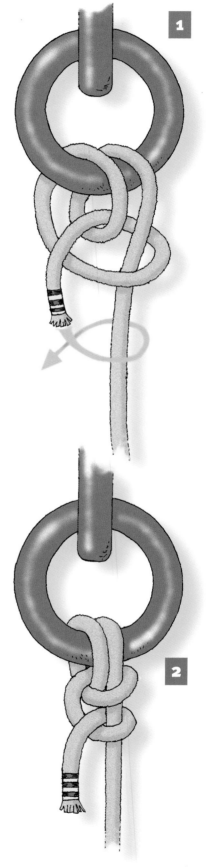

DOUBLE OVERHAND KNOT

Purpose

This makes a bulkier stopper knot than the basic overhand knot, and is often preferred for that reason—but note that, contrary to what is often said, it will *not* block a larger hole or slot. If a larger knot is required, use Ashley's stopper knot (*page 29*).

Tying

Tie an overhand knot and tuck the working end a second time (*figures 1–2*). Pull carefully on both ends at the same time and feel how the two helixing knot parts tend to unwind, imparting their twist to the single knot part. Encourage this transformation by twisting both standing parts in opposite directions as shown (*figure 3*). Finally pull the knot tight (*figure 4*). This technique should be mastered as it is indispensable for other knots that rely upon it.

Twist...

Twist...

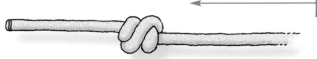

STRANGLE KNOT

Purpose

This is a binding knot, for use in jobs as diverse as seizing a hose pipe to a water source, holding a roll of carpet, or embellishing a presentation scroll.

Tying

Tie a double overhand knot and slide it over the object as shown (*figure 1*). Pull as tight as required (*figure 2*). It will also hold together a coil of rope (*figure 3*) so that it might be carried on the shoulder or slung diagonally across one's chest.

Knot lore

In his book *Om Knutar* (1916) the Swedish knot expert Hjalmar Öhrvall preferred this knot to the constrictor knot (*pages 94–95*) because its turns bedded down more snugly together. In the March 1997 issue of *Knotting Matters* (the quarterly magazine of the International Guild of Knot Tyers), a contributor writing under the pen-name of Jack Fidspike confirmed:

> The Bag, Sack or Miller's knots
> Are rudimentary bindings,
> But often ropework jobs need lots
> Of more elaborate windings.
> The aptly named Constrictor
> Will cling and grip like glue, Sir!
> While the Strangle knot's a stricture
> Some deem neater—and no looser.

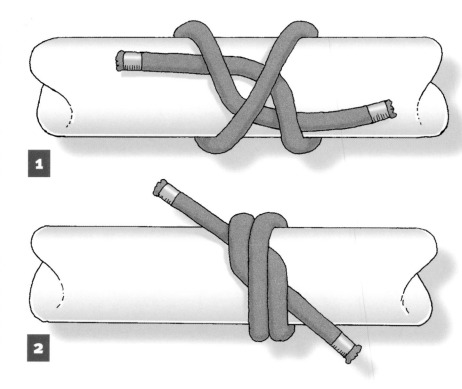

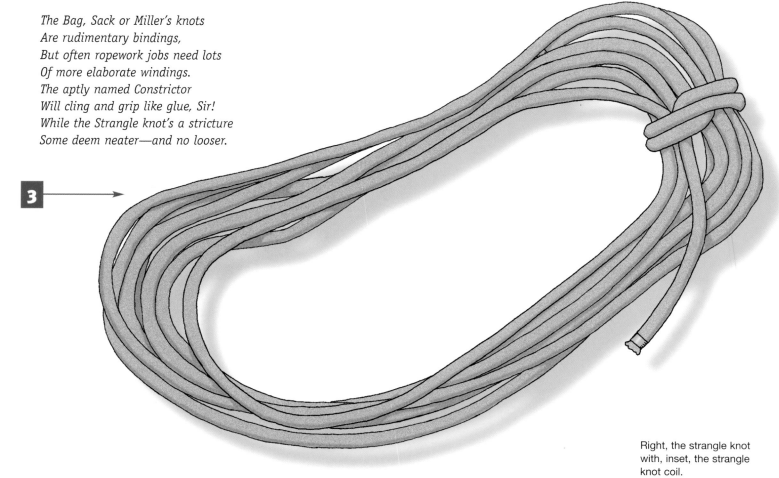

Right, the strangle knot with, inset, the strangle knot coil.

& STRANGLE KNOT COIL

DOUBLE OVERHAND NOOSE

Purpose

This is a stronger and more secure alternative to the simple overhand noose, better suited to larger cordage.

Tying

Make a long-ish bight in the end of the line (*figure 1*) and with the working end tie a double overhand knot around the adjacent standing part (*figures 2–3*). Pull the knot tight and slide it along to adjust the loop to the required size (*figure 4*).

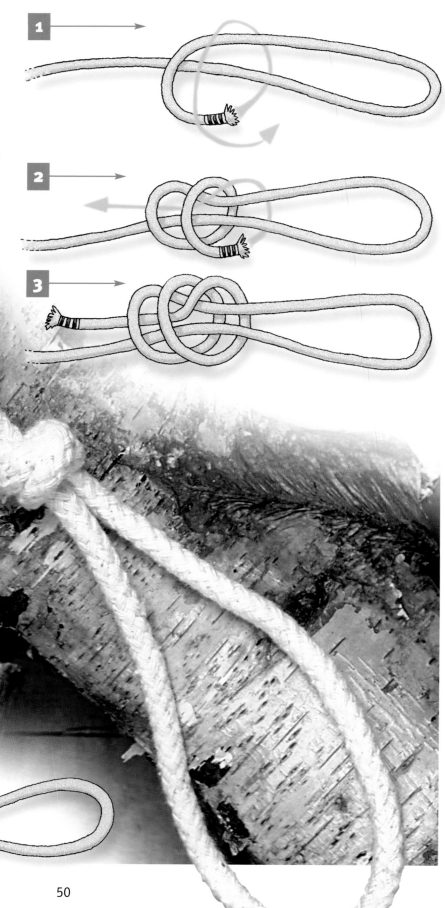

DOUBLE FISHERMAN'S KNOT

1

2

3

Purpose

Use this knot as a stronger and more secure alternative to the basic fisherman's knot (*pages 34–35*). As such, it is better suited to smooth synthetic cordage as well as thin monofilaments.

Tying

Bring the two lines together, parallel, with ends pointing in opposite directions. Tie a double overhand knot with one end around the adjacent standing part (*figure 1*). Tie an identical knot (that is, of the same handedness) with the other end around its nearby standing part and pull the two knots together (*figures 2–3*).

Knot lore

Anglers know this knot as a grinner knot, presumably because of the gaping mouth that can be created between the two knots prior to pulling them shut.

DOUBLE OVERHAND LOOP

Purpose

This makes a strong fixed loop for thinner stuff but not for rope (as it jams).

Tying

Form a long bight and tie an overhand knot in the doubled end of the line, then take an extra tuck (*figure 1*). Coax the knot into shape, tightening it a bit at a time, taking care to arrange each turn so that it will lie snugly without parallel tracks (*figure 2*) and only then tension and tighten it (*figure 3*).

SECTION 2
FIGURE OF EIGHT KNOTS

When you get to the end of your rope, tie a knot and hang on."
Franklin D. Roosevelt, 32nd President of the USA, 1933–45)

The figure of eight layout is a versatile one for knot tying and, like the ubiquitous overhand knot, appears repeatedly on the knotting scene. Cavers and climbers prefer knots based upon it because they are more easily learned, tied in all sorts of situations, (when there is the likelihood of other knots being done wrongly due to fear or fatigue), and readily checked by team leaders.

In 1999 in England, the Surrey Branch of the International Guild of Knot Tyers published what a consensus of its members considered were the six knots that should be used with modern ropes. They were: the figure of eight; sheet bend; bowline; constrictor; rolling hitch; and a round turn and two half-hitches. All of these knots are featured in this book. While other knotting devotees might discuss amiably all day whether or not they agreed with this selection, the Surrey Branch went further and urged that the figure of eight knot (which can be modified to act as a loop, bend, hitch and stopper knot) ought to be taught first of all.

FIGURE OF EIGHT KNOT

Purpose

The basic knot is a stopper knot. It is easily untied after use and is recommended for any rope work that will be repeatedly assembled and dismantled. Note that, despite its bulkier appearance, it will *not* stop up a larger hole or slot than either the overhand or double overhand knots. As advised earlier, if a larger stopper knot is needed, use Ashley's stopper knot.

Tying

Make a loop and impart an extra twist (*figure 1*). Tuck the working end as shown to create the characteristic figure of eight layout that gives this family of knots its name (*figures 2–3*). Tighten the knot, taking care to push the bight furthest from the end of the line up as far as it will go, while at the same time pulling down on the standing part of the line to bend and trap the working end (*figure 4*).

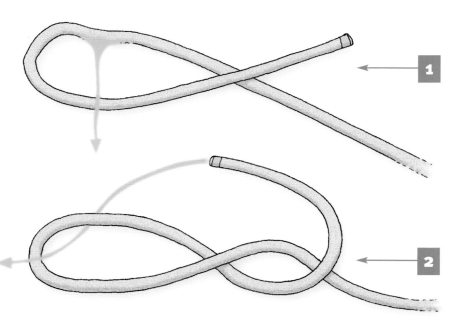

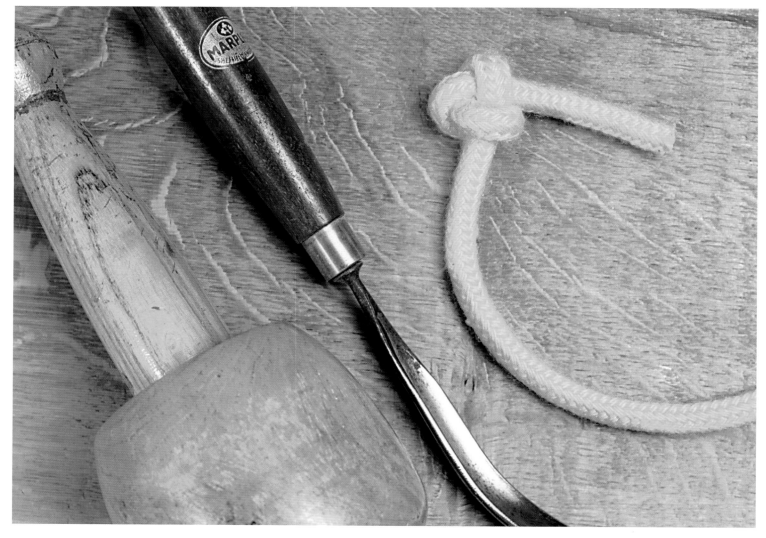

When only the most temporary use will be made of this knot, consider incorporating a quick-release draw-loop (*figure 5*).

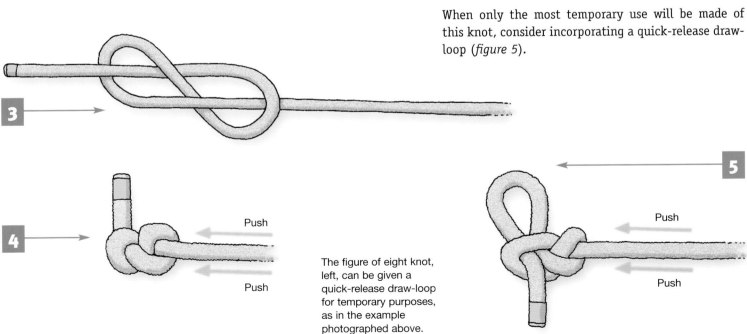

3

4

The figure of eight knot, left, can be given a quick-release draw-loop for temporary purposes, as in the example photographed above.

Push

Push

5

Push

Push

FIGURE OF EIGHT NOOSE

Purpose

This creates a basic adjustable loop and may be used as an alternative to the double overhand noose.

Tying

Make a loop and then wrap and tuck the working end in a figure of eight as shown (*figures 1–3*). Pull the knot tight so that it closes up into a more compact form (*figure 4*).

Knot lore

Nooses in general were used in previous centuries, to snare game, small birds and vermin. These days they are for starting lashings and tying packages with string. Clifford Ashley in his monumental *Book of Knots* (1944) awards this one a five-pointed star to signify that, of all the simple nooses, he rated it *Best for the Purpose*.

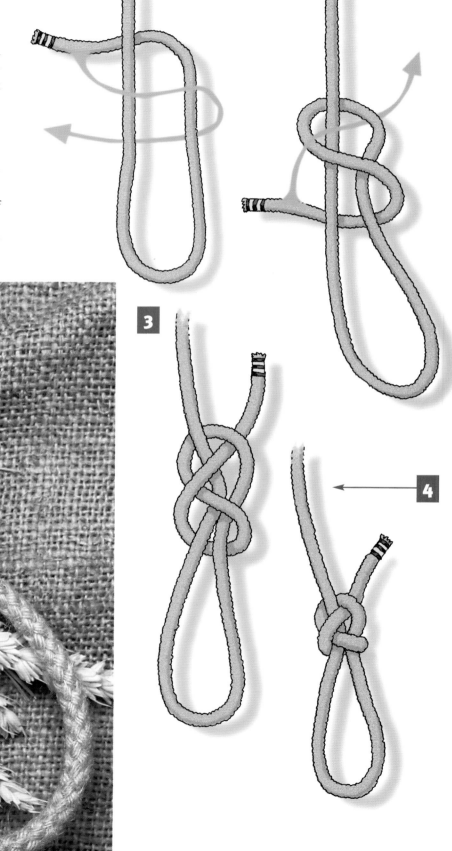

FIGURE OF EIGHT HITCH

Purpose

Use this simple hitch for attaching any light line to an anchorage point.

Tying

Take a turn around the rail, post, ring or other fixture and then wrap and tuck the working end as shown (*figures 1–2*). Finally pull what is in effect a sliding loop snug and tight (*figure 3*).

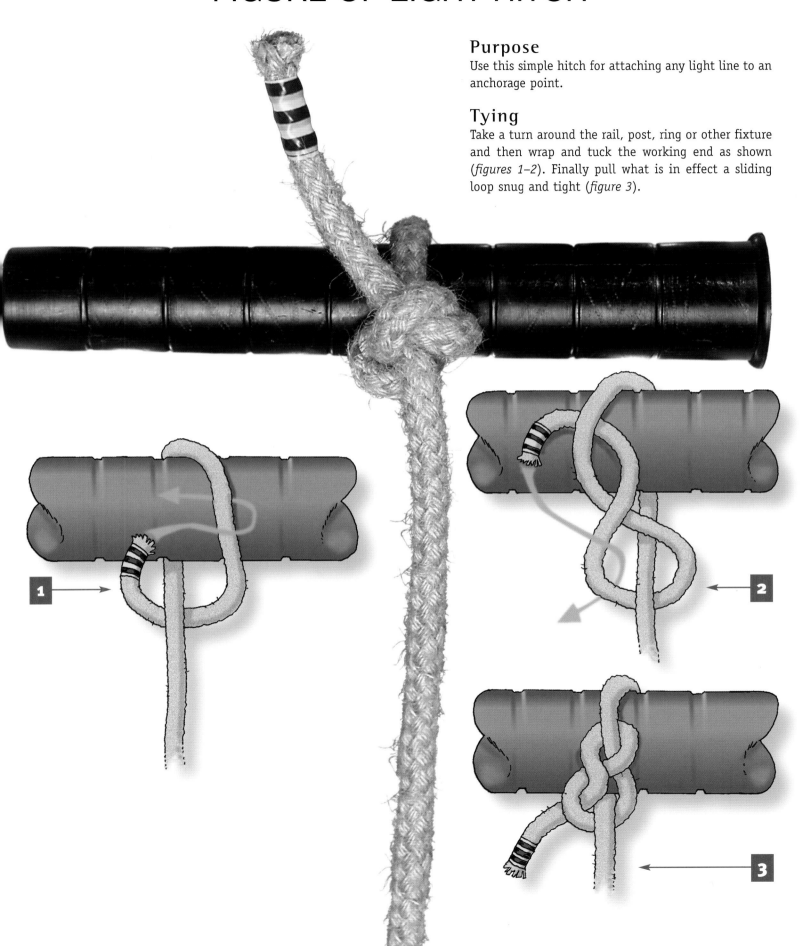

FIGURE OF EIGHT LOOP

Purpose

A strong and secure all-purpose fixed loop, it will hold in the finest threads but is also suitable for working ropes (and can be undone after use).

Tying

Make a long bight and tie a figure of eight knot in the loop so formed (*figures 1–3*). Remove unsightly twisted knot parts and rearrange the layout with crossovers at each end of the knot to streamline it when it is pulled tight (*figure 4*).

Knot lore

The older name for this knot was a Flemish loop.

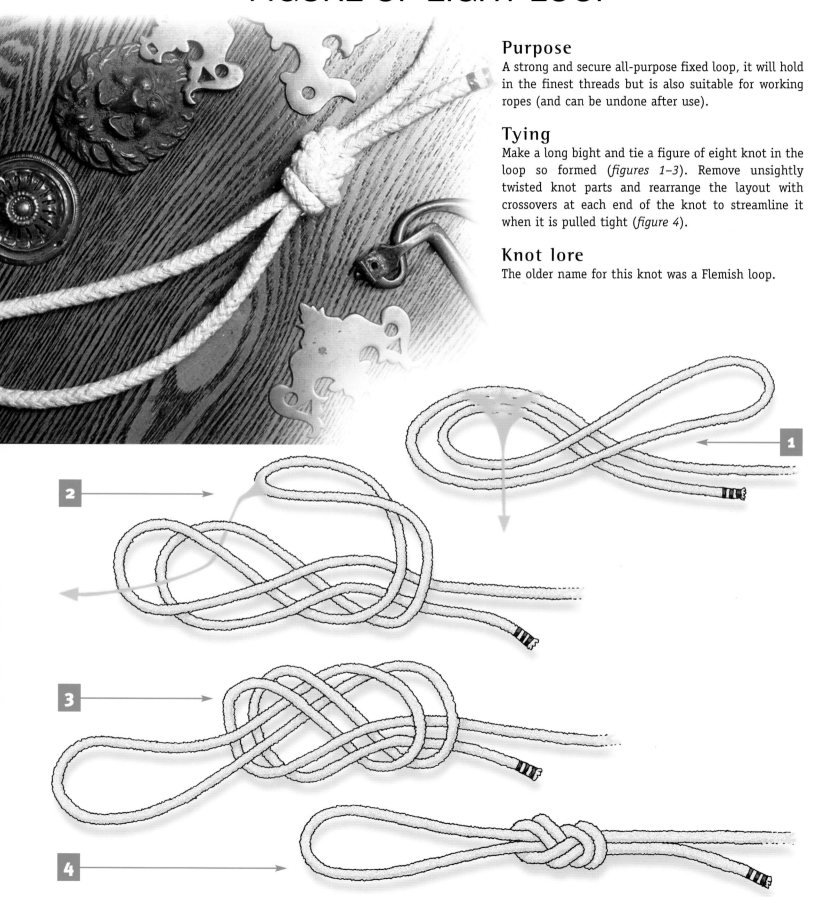

FIGURE OF EIGHT BECKET HITCH

1

2

3

Purpose
To neatly fasten a line to a permanent loop, seized eye or becket, use this knot.

Tying
Pass the working end of the line through the becket or other loop, then wrap and tuck as shown (*figures 1–3*).

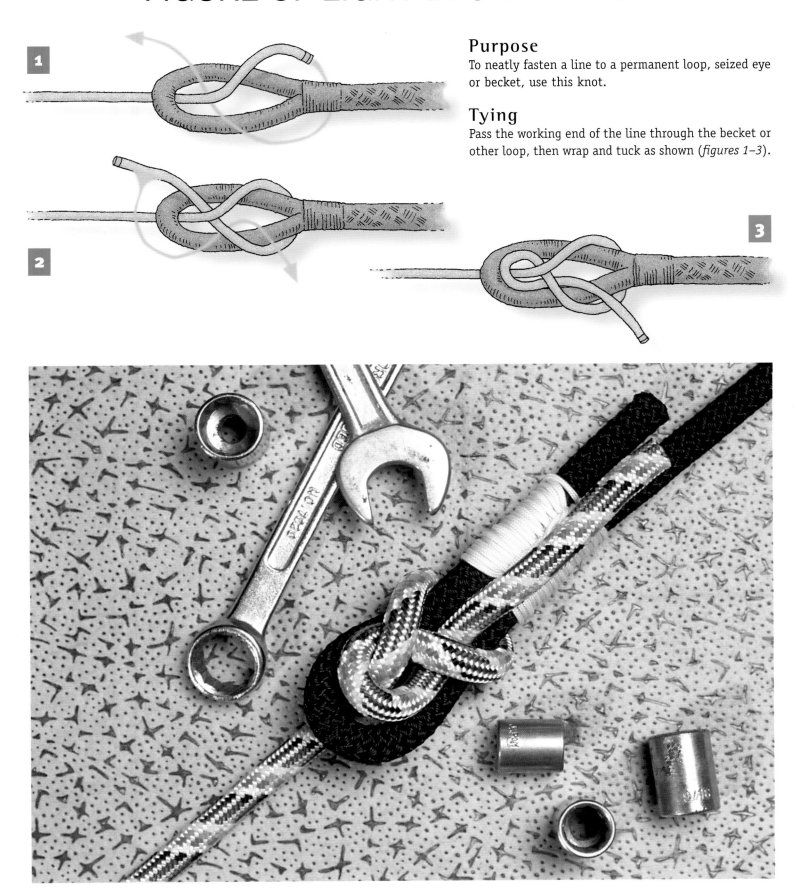

SLIDING FIGURE OF EIGHT BEND

Purpose

This is a strong bend for the largest ropes, although it can also be used on smaller cordage. It is preferable to the fisherman's knot (*pages 34–35*) when ease of untying after use is a desirable characteristic.

Tying

Marry the two lines to be joined, parallel and close together, with ends in opposite directions. Then tie a figure of eight knot in one end and introduce the other end (*figure 1*). Tie a second identical figure of eight knot with the other end around its nearby standing part (*figures 2–3*). Tighten both knots and then pull them together (*figure 4*).

Knot lore

The older name for this knot was Flemish bend.

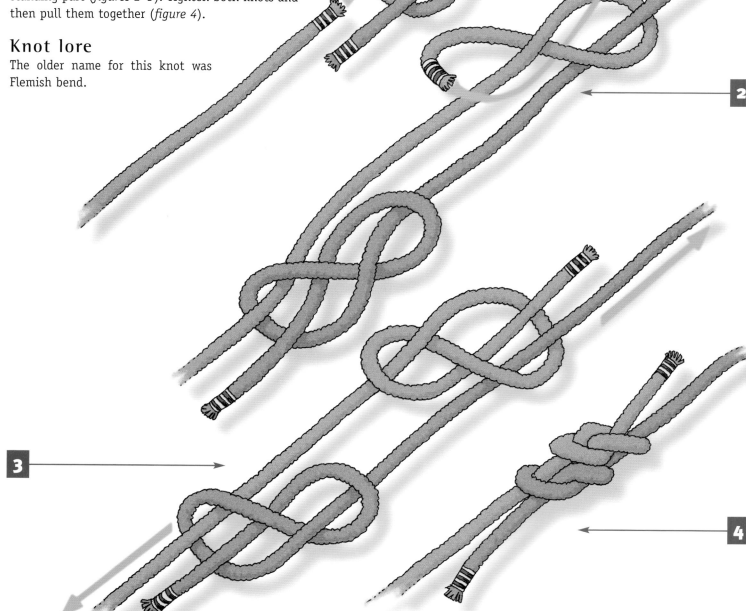

FIGURE OF EIGHT BEND

Purpose
This version of a figure of eight bend is not so readily untied after use, but is somewhat more streamlined that the preceding one.

Tying
Tie a figure of eight knot in one line, then introduce the working end of the other (*figure 1*). Follow around the lead of the original knot until it has been duplicated (*figure 2*), and then carefully tighten the composite knot (*figure 3*).

Knot lore
Another of the so-called Flemish bends, Clifford Ashley reported that it was bulky and bothersome to tie.

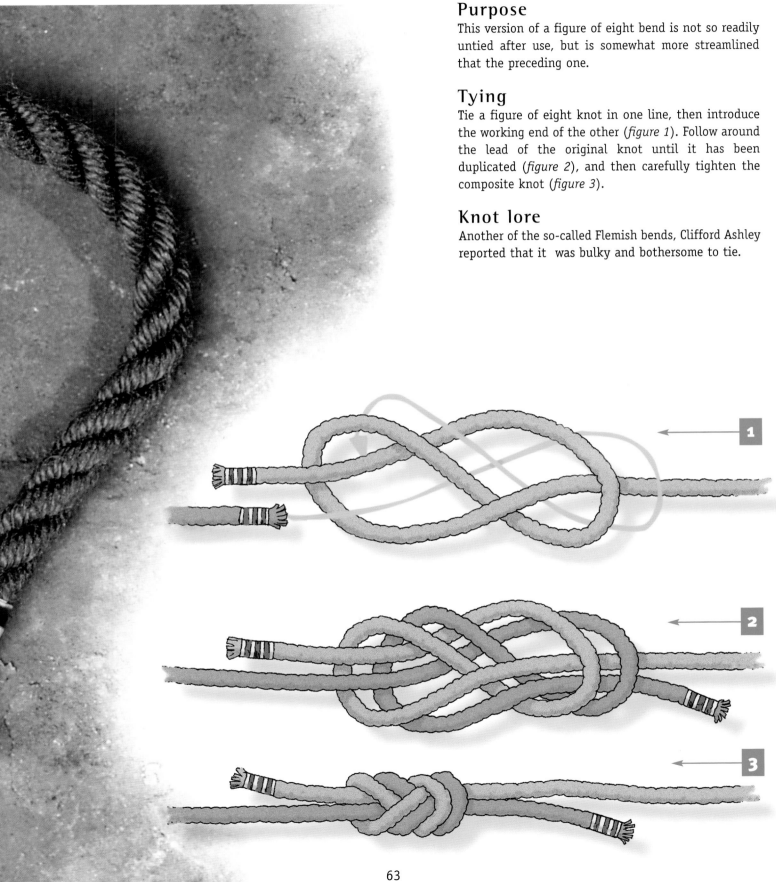

FIGURE OF EIGHT TWIN LOOPS

Purpose

Twin loop knots are generally portrayed as *ad hoc* chair slings for working—ashore or afloat—while seated in one loop, with the other around one's armpits at chest height. Alternatively, they were designed to rescue an injured person by raising or lowering them. If conscious, the patient might thrust a leg through each loop and hold on above the knot. Either way, the support is very uncomfortable.

Nowadays hazardous working practices are generally outlawed and the authorities charged with monitoring health and safety are prepared to prosecute any foreseeable risk-taking. Similarly, victims of any recklessness or carelessness are all too willing to sue those responsible for their loss, injury or damage. Consequently I do not recommend the regular use of these knots as rescue or chair slings. There are harnesses, properly tested and certificated, for such purposes. For all who would be prepared for that rare occasion when an improvised rope sling may still be justified, however, this knot is one that would serve.

Tying

Make a long bight and in the resulting doubled line tie a figure of eight knot with a draw-loop (*figures 1–2*). Bring the single projecting loop down in front of the incomplete knot, lifting the two other loops forward through it, and then replace it upward behind the body of the knot (*figure 3*). Then carefully tighten everything (*figure 4*).

Knot lore

This knot seems to have been first described and illustrated by Clifford Ashley in *The Ashley Book of Knots* (1944).

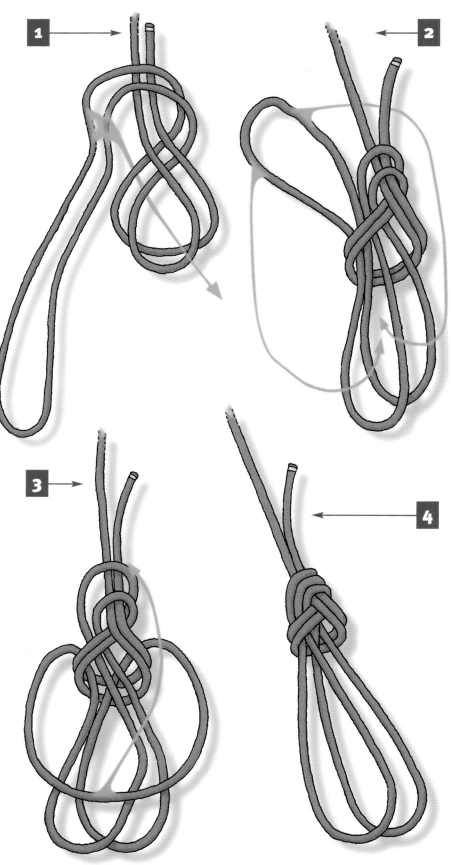

FIGURE OF EIGHT TRIPLE LOOP

Purpose

This chair sling knot provides a loop for each leg and another to go around beneath the armpits at chest height—but see the caution given for the similar knot on the previous page.

Tying

First make a long bight and with the doubled line begin by tying a figure of eight knot with a draw-loop (*figure 1*). Then bring the projecting single loop up and over the front of the knot to be tucked as shown. Tighten the numerous knot parts, at the same time adjusting the loops to the size required (*figure 2*).

Knot lore

This knot was first described and illustrated in the mid-1980s by the accomplished Canadian climber Robert Chisnall, who later served as President (1996–98) of the International Guild of Knot Tyers.

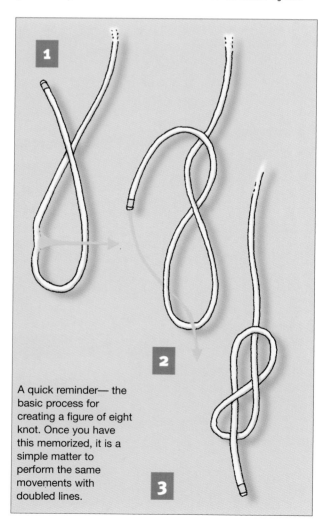

A quick reminder— the basic process for creating a figure of eight knot. Once you have this memorized, it is a simple matter to perform the same movements with doubled lines.

FIGURE OF EIGHT COIL

Purpose

This is a quick way to coil a rope prior to hanging it up, either for long-term storage or simply to keep it temporarily out from underfoot in a working area (since it can be quickly freed for re-use).

Tying

Middle the rope (that is, find the midway point and double it), then coil it, right-handed (clockwise) if the rope is laid right-handed, starting at the bight and working toward the two ends (*figure 1*). Wrap and tuck the bight as shown (*figure 2*) and arrange the coils so that they are held snugly but not too tightly by the enclosing figure of eight layout (*figure 3*).

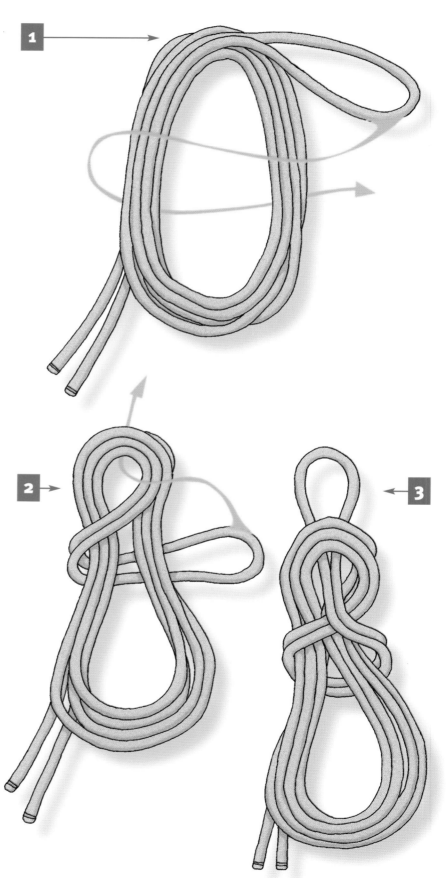

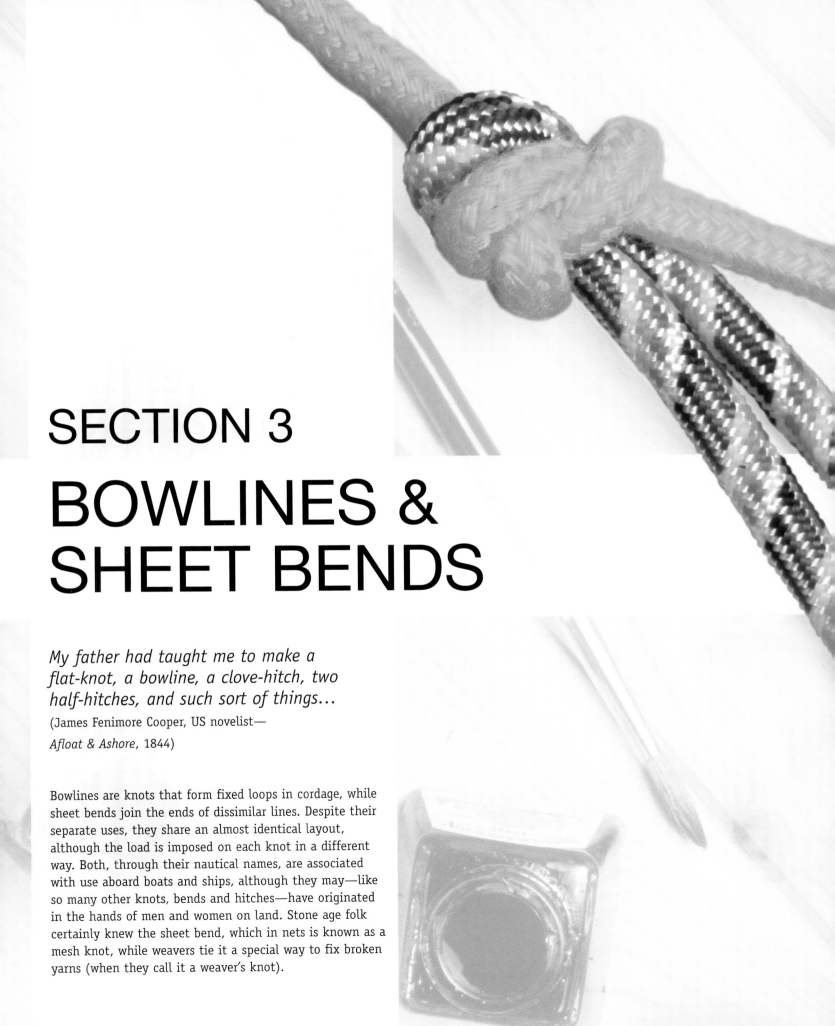

SECTION 3
BOWLINES & SHEET BENDS

My father had taught me to make a flat-knot, a bowline, a clove-hitch, two half-hitches, and such sort of things...

(James Fenimore Cooper, US novelist—

Afloat & Ashore, 1844)

Bowlines are knots that form fixed loops in cordage, while sheet bends join the ends of dissimilar lines. Despite their separate uses, they share an almost identical layout, although the load is imposed on each knot in a different way. Both, through their nautical names, are associated with use aboard boats and ships, although they may—like so many other knots, bends and hitches—have originated in the hands of men and women on land. Stone age folk certainly knew the sheet bend, which in nets is known as a mesh knot, while weavers tie it a special way to fix broken yarns (when they call it a weaver's knot).

COMMON BOWLINE

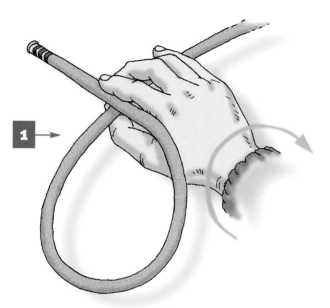

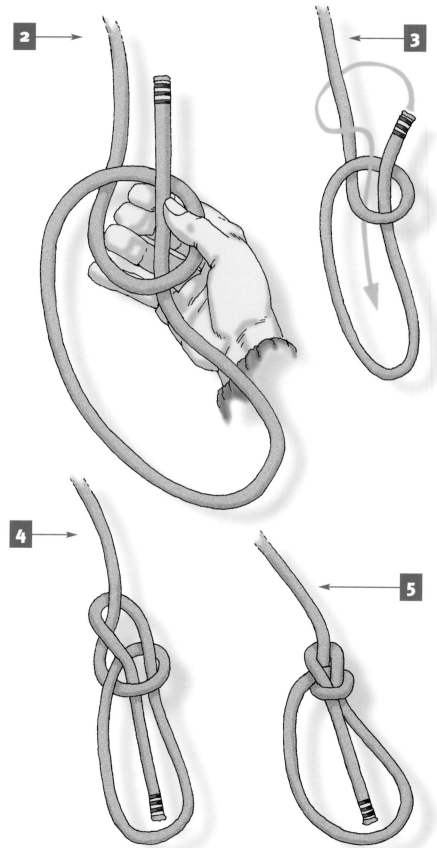

Purpose

Pronounced *boh-linn*, the common bowline forms a single fixed loop. It is a classic knot but neither strong (about 60%) nor very secure unless the tail end is taped or tied to its adjacent loop leg.

Tying

Make a loop and grasp it in one hand (palm down), then turn that hand palm up to trip or roll a loop into the standing part, through which the working end is automatically inserted (*figures 1–2*). Tuck the working end as indicated to complete this knot (*figures 3–4*). In tightening the knot ensure that the tail end is as long as a moderate sized loop.

Knot lore

At sea the bow line was a rope used to hold the weather leech of a square sail forward closer to the wind, to prevent it from being taken aback (that is, unintentionally blown inside out, impeding the ship's progress), so the knot that secured it was literally a bow line knot; but it has since become diminished, and its pronunciation altered.

A.P. (later Sir Alan) Herbert, the English playwright, lyricist and wit—and Member of Parliament for the University of Oxford, when that academic and august institution had its own parliamentary representative—wrote in his poem *The Bowline* that it was the King of Knots, and many knot tyers (some unaware of the source) still use that sobriquet.

TWIN BOWLINE BEND

Purpose

A neat way to join two large ropes or cables—or indeed smaller cordage—so that they may readily be untied after use, is to link a couple of bowlines in this way.

Tying

Lay the two working ends alongside one another, parallel and pointing in opposite directions. Make a loop in one standing part and tuck the working end of the other line to complete the knot. Do the same with the other end. Ensure that both knots are adjusted so that any load falls equally on both legs of line between the two knots.

WATER BOWLINE

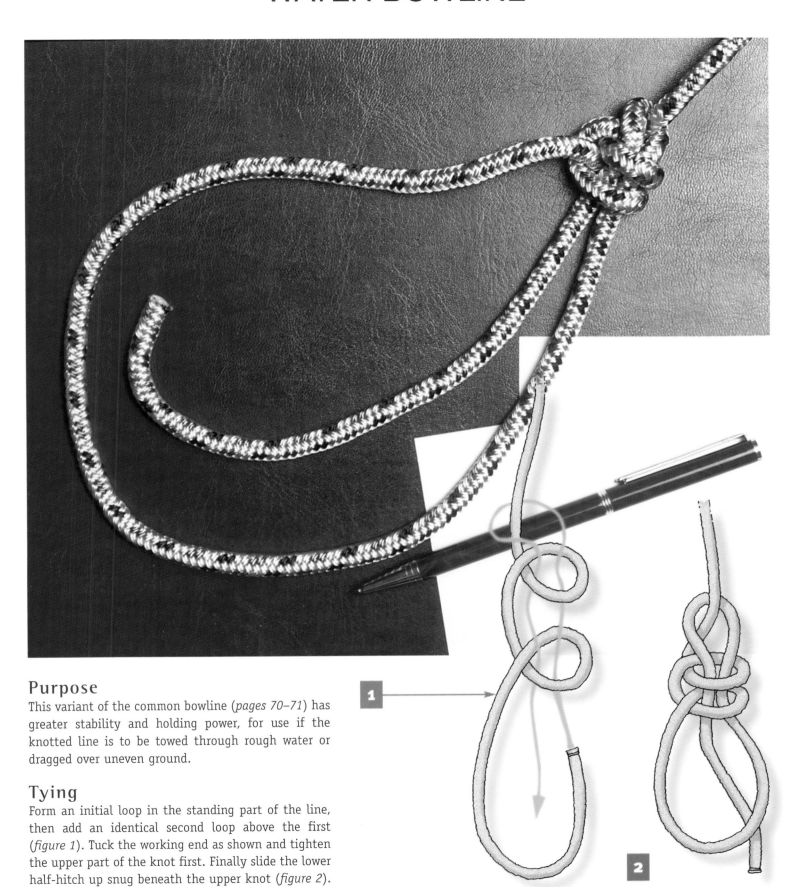

Purpose

This variant of the common bowline (*pages 70–71*) has greater stability and holding power, for use if the knotted line is to be towed through rough water or dragged over uneven ground.

Tying

Form an initial loop in the standing part of the line, then add an identical second loop above the first (*figure 1*). Tuck the working end as shown and tighten the upper part of the knot first. Finally slide the lower half-hitch up snug beneath the upper knot (*figure 2*).

1

2

DOUBLE BOWLINE

Purpose

The extra wrapping turn of this knot—similar in layout to a double sheet bend (*page 82*) adds strength and security. It is this doubled cinch around the bight of the working end that has given this knot its misleading name, since it does *not* have twin loops. When such a knot is required, use the bowline in the bight.

Tying

Overlap two identical loops and tuck the working end through both as shown (*figure 1*). Tighten the knot (*figure 2*).

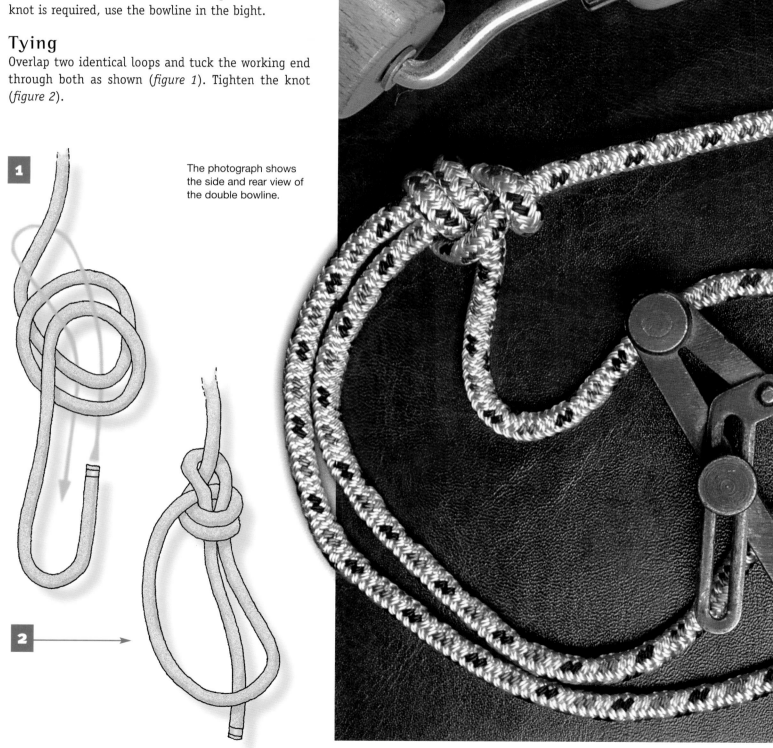

1

The photograph shows the side and rear view of the double bowline.

2

BOWLINE IN THE BIGHT

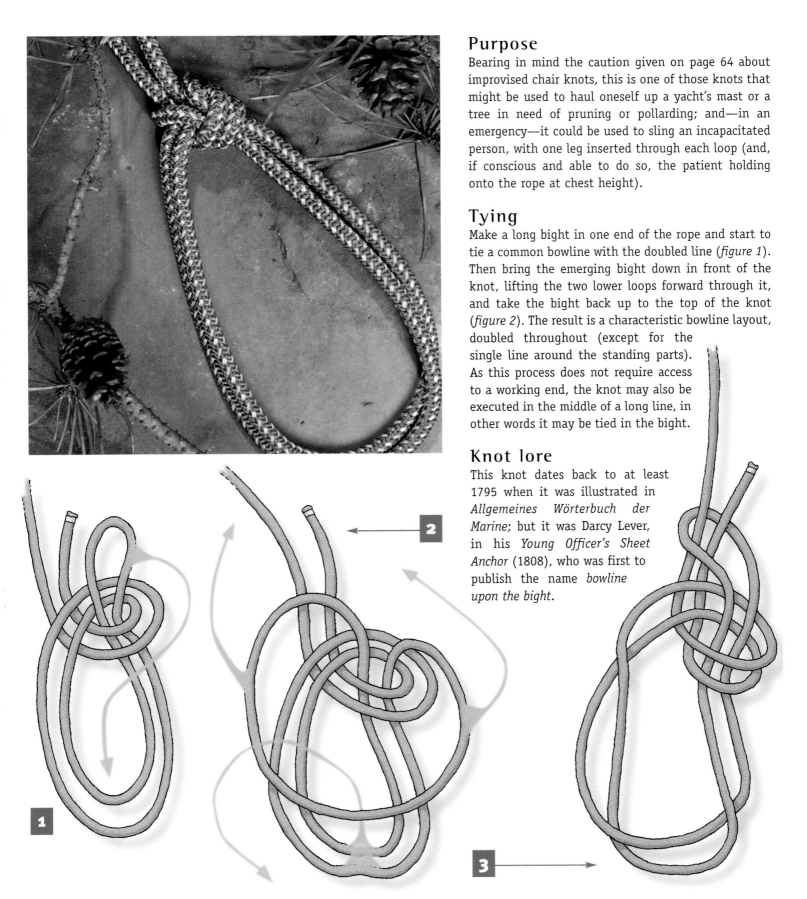

Purpose
Bearing in mind the caution given on page 64 about improvised chair knots, this is one of those knots that might be used to haul oneself up a yacht's mast or a tree in need of pruning or pollarding; and—in an emergency—it could be used to sling an incapacitated person, with one leg inserted through each loop (and, if conscious and able to do so, the patient holding onto the rope at chest height).

Tying
Make a long bight in one end of the rope and start to tie a common bowline with the doubled line (*figure 1*). Then bring the emerging bight down in front of the knot, lifting the two lower loops forward through it, and take the bight back up to the top of the knot (*figure 2*). The result is a characteristic bowline layout, doubled throughout (except for the single line around the standing parts). As this process does not require access to a working end, the knot may also be executed in the middle of a long line, in other words it may be tied in the bight.

Knot lore
This knot dates back to at least 1795 when it was illustrated in *Allgemeines Wörterbuch der Marine*; but it was Darcy Lever, in his *Young Officer's Sheet Anchor* (1808), who was first to publish the name *bowline upon the bight*.

TRIPLE BOWLINE

Purpose

Recalling my earlier caution about improvised chair knots, this will accommodate a leg through each loop and provides a third one to go around the person's chest beneath their armpits. Each loop must be painstakingly adjusted to the right size.

Tying

Make a long bight in the rope and simply tie a common bowline with the doubled portion of line (*figures 1–2*). As no end is involved, this is another of those handy knots that is tied in the bight.

Knot lore

The triple bowline was shown me by the Canadian climber Robert Chisnall.

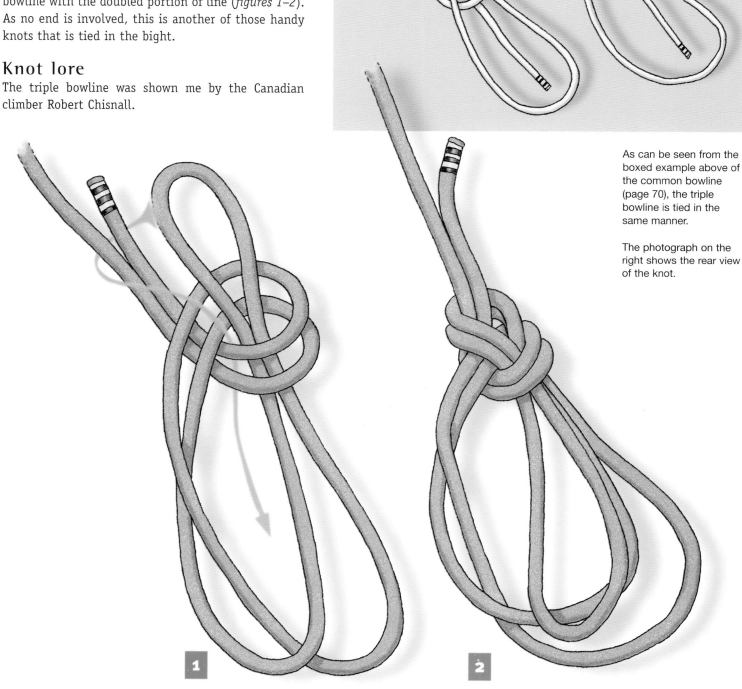

As can be seen from the boxed example above of the common bowline (page 70), the triple bowline is tied in the same manner.

The photograph on the right shows the rear view of the knot.

ESKIMO BOWLINE

Purpose

Quickly and easily tied, this unorthodox bowline is more secure and may be used in situations where the regular knot would shake loose and spill. It could pass for the tricorn loop (*pages 32–33*), already described in Section 1—Overhand Knots, but in fact it has one less crossing point.

Tying

Begin as if for an overhand knot, but then interweave the working end over-under-over as shown (*figure 1*). Pull upon the two knot parts indicated to transform the knot (*figures 2–3*) when a sort of bowline-on-its-side results. Tighten it and a compact tricorn button knot appears (*figure 4*).

Knot lore

Early in 1985 I was invited to visit London's Museum of Mankind to examine an Inuit sled, a jig-saw of bone and ivory bits and pieces, lashed together with rawhide thongs. Each lashing sported what appeared to be little triangular buttons knots, which it took me a while to work out were actually these bowlines used as hitches to begin each lashing.

The earliest previous use of this knot (on Baffin Island) was recorded by the ethnologist Franz Boas, in 1907, and for that reason it has been referred to as the Boas bowline. But the sled I saw had been presented to polar explorer Sir John Ross (1777–1856) at an earlier date, by a tribe of Inuits, and it was old when they gave it to him. Moreover, they had not seen a white man before. So, not only can the inference be made that this knot has a genuine Inuit pedigree (rather than being a common bowline copied, wrongly, from European seaman) but it is perhaps 100 years older than the sighting by Boas.

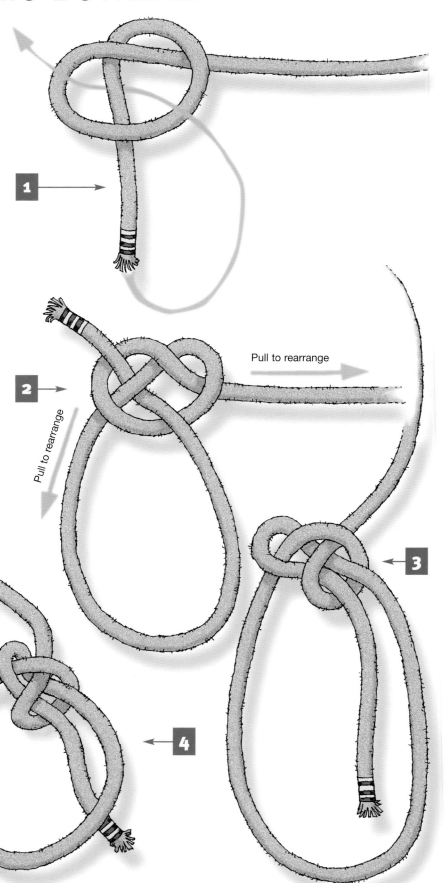

Pull to rearrange

Pull to rearrange

SHEET BEND

Purpose

Use this knot to join two lines together, or a line to a loop of some kind (when it is called a becket hitch). It will also cope with two lengths of cordage of somewhat dissimilar size and construction, in which case the bight must be made in the larger or stiffer material.

Tying

Form a bight in one end and insert the other through it (*figure 1*). Wrap and tuck the working end as shown, taking care that both ends emerge on the same side of the knot (*figure 2*) since the knot seems in some materials to be more secure that way. Tighten it (*figure 3*). For a temporary hold-fast, and a quick-release, incorporate a draw-loop (*figure 4*).

Knot lore

Remnants of nets from the Neolithic period have been found with mesh knots that resemble sheet bends.

A "sheet" was—and still is—a rope that controls or trims the lower corner of a sail (to "sheet home" or "sheet flat" is to pull the sheet taut, and so haul in the sail), from which comes the name sheet bend. David Steel used the name sheet bend in his *Elements and Practice of Rigging and Seamanship* (1794).

Some knot experts campaign against the use of this bend for lines of different sizes, pointing out that (if they are too dissimilar) a thick and stiff rope could overcome its weaker partner, straighten out and spill the knot. While this is a valid concern, it would be throwing the baby out with the bath water to discard this knot (since the property of accommodating dissimilar lines is a useful one). Knot craftsman and writer Stuart E. Grainger struck the right note:

> Use a Sheet Bend
> To join on an end
> To another of different size;
> Also to tie through a thimble or eye,
> But insure against trouble,
> Tie it double.

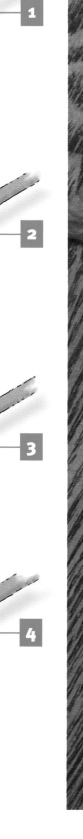

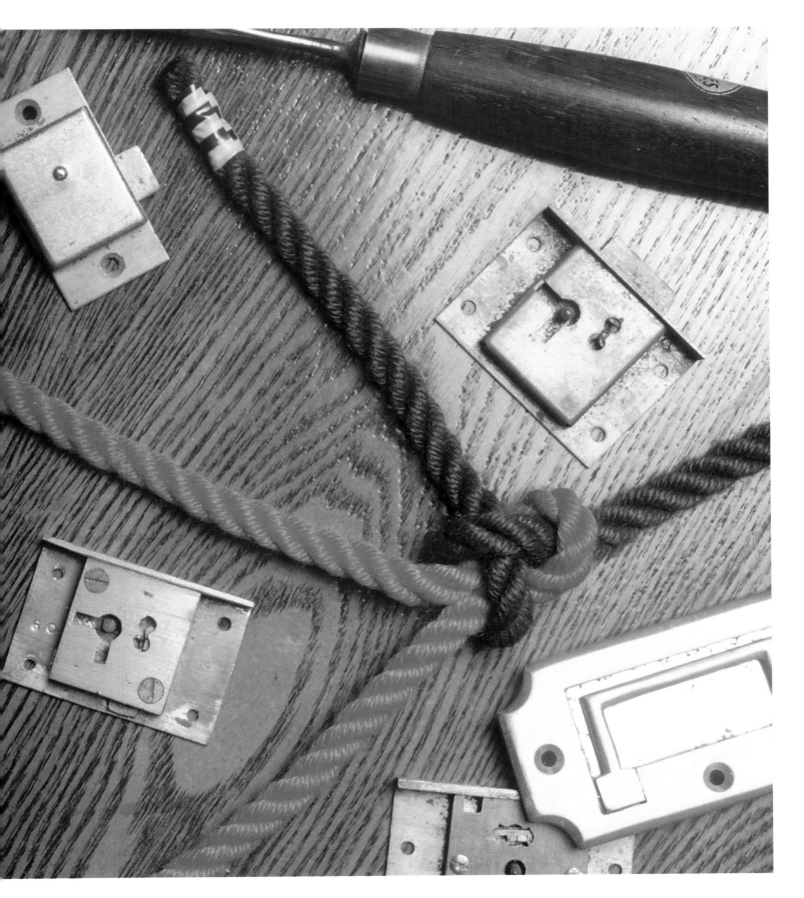

DOUBLE SHEET BEND

Purpose

This is the reinforced knot hinted at by Stuart Grainger in his cautionary verse (*see the previous page*), for use when a common sheet bend might have a tendency to slip or spill. It is similar in design to the double bowline (*page 74*).

Tying

Tie a common sheet bend and then tuck the working end a second time (*figure 1*). Ensure both wrapping turns lie neatly alongside one another and then tighten the knot (*figures 2–3*).

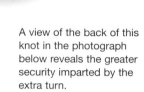

A view of the back of this knot in the photograph below reveals the greater security imparted by the extra turn.

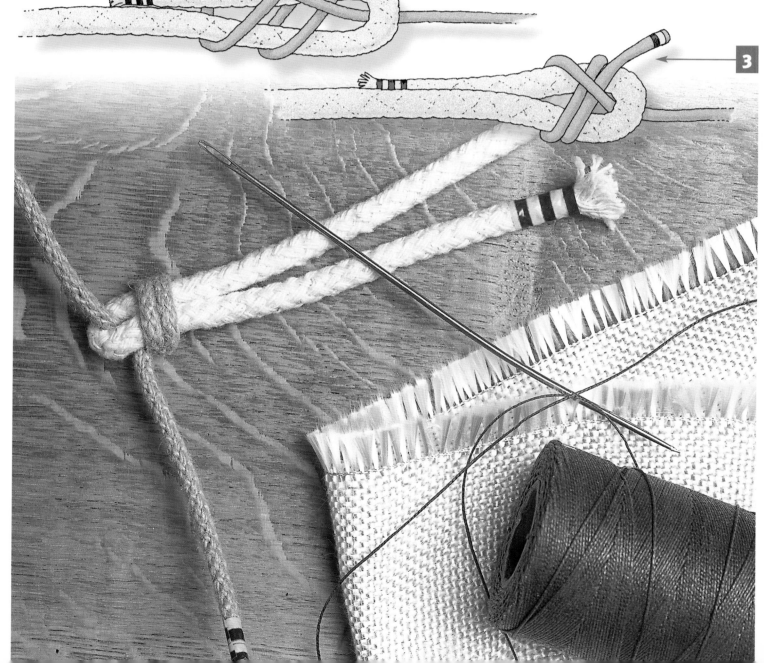

ONE-WAY SHEET BEND

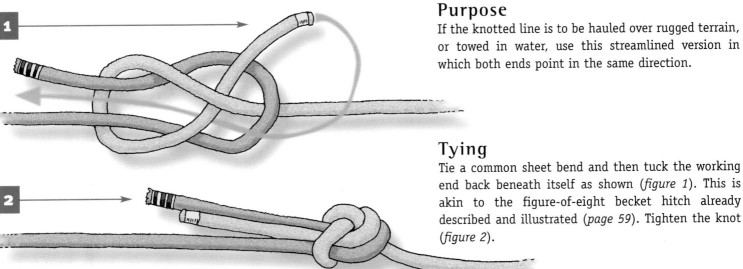

Purpose
If the knotted line is to be hauled over rugged terrain, or towed in water, use this streamlined version in which both ends point in the same direction.

Tying
Tie a common sheet bend and then tuck the working end back beneath itself as shown (*figure 1*). This is akin to the figure-of-eight becket hitch already described and illustrated (*page 59*). Tighten the knot (*figure 2*).

THREE-WAY SHEET BEND

Purpose
This adaptation of the common sheet bend (*pages 80–81*) will act as a neat bridle to secure and hold three converging lines.

Tying
Make a bight in the thickest or stiffest of the three lines, then tie a sheet bend layout with the other two.

Knot lore
Swedish yachting writer Frank Rosenow, a member of the International Guild of Knot Tyers, spotted this unorthodox application of the sheet bend while cruising in Greek waters and reported it in his book *Seagoing Knots* (1990).

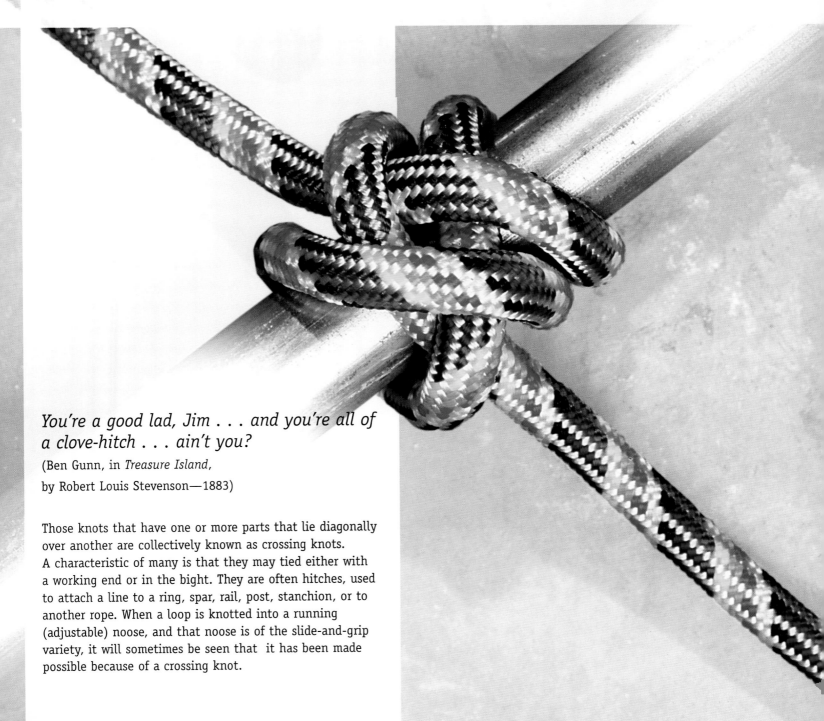

SECTION 4
CROSSING KNOTS

You're a good lad, Jim . . . and you're all of a clove-hitch . . . ain't you?
(Ben Gunn, in *Treasure Island*,
by Robert Louis Stevenson—1883)

Those knots that have one or more parts that lie diagonally over another are collectively known as crossing knots. A characteristic of many is that they may tied either with a working end or in the bight. They are often hitches, used to attach a line to a ring, spar, rail, post, stanchion, or to another rope. When a loop is knotted into a running (adjustable) noose, and that noose is of the slide-and-grip variety, it will sometimes be seen that it has been made possible because of a crossing knot.

CLOVE HITCH

Purpose

The simplicity of this much-used hitch limits its application, for it can be trusted only as long as the pull is a steady one from a direction that is mostly at right-angles to the point of attachment. Otherwise it can prove unreliable. Provided this shortcoming is borne in mind, however, it is a knot worth knowing, one that can be tied by several different methods (the two most handy ones being described below).

Tying #1

Take a turn with the working end around the intended anchorage and then cross over the standing part of the line (*figure 1*). Tuck as shown (*figure 2*). To suspend items by a lanyard—from a fender on a boat to a string of onions in the cellar—leave a draw-loop for later easy release (*figure 3*).

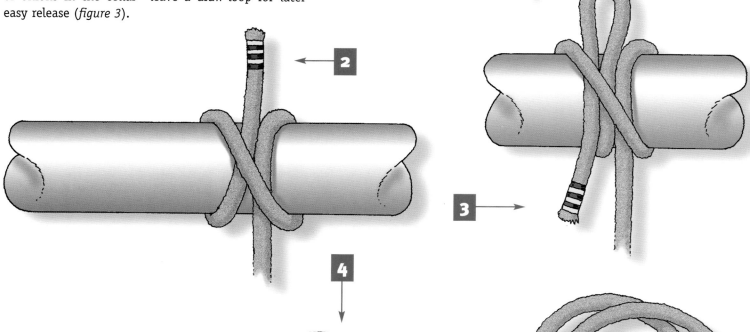

Tying #2

To tie this knot quickly and simply in the bight—even when a working end is available—form a pair of alternate loops and overlap them (*figure 4*), then slip the resulting layout over the post or other point of attachment (*figure 5*).

Knot lore

On land this was once known as the builder's knot. The name clove hitch seems to have been published first in the *Universal Dictionary of the Marine* (1769) by William Falconer.

BUNTLINE HITCH

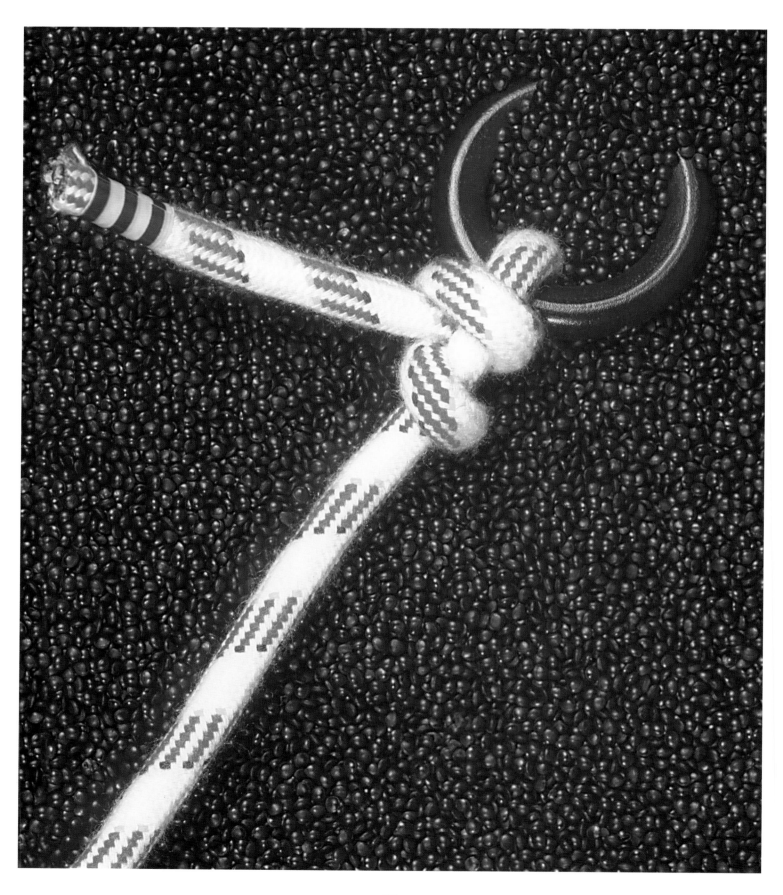

Purpose

This is one of those nooses that is actually employed as a hitch. Use it to attach a line to a ring or other item of hardware that is likely to be shaken violently about (such as the metal clips on a flag halyard). Do not use it for jobs that will require it to be untied quickly because, with the final tuck trapped within the knot, it is prone to jam—which is what is required of this knot.

Tying

Tie what is in effect a clove hitch with the working end around the standing part of the line (*figures 1–2*). Tighten the resulting knot tight and then pull the loop shut (*figure 3*).

Knot lore

Aboard large sailing ships, this knot was used to attach a rope called a buntline to the foot-rope of a topsail. This line passed up in front of the sail to a block on the yard and was used to pull the bottom of the sail up and so spill the wind out of it. In the process canvas and cordage shook violently, so a very secure knot was needed.

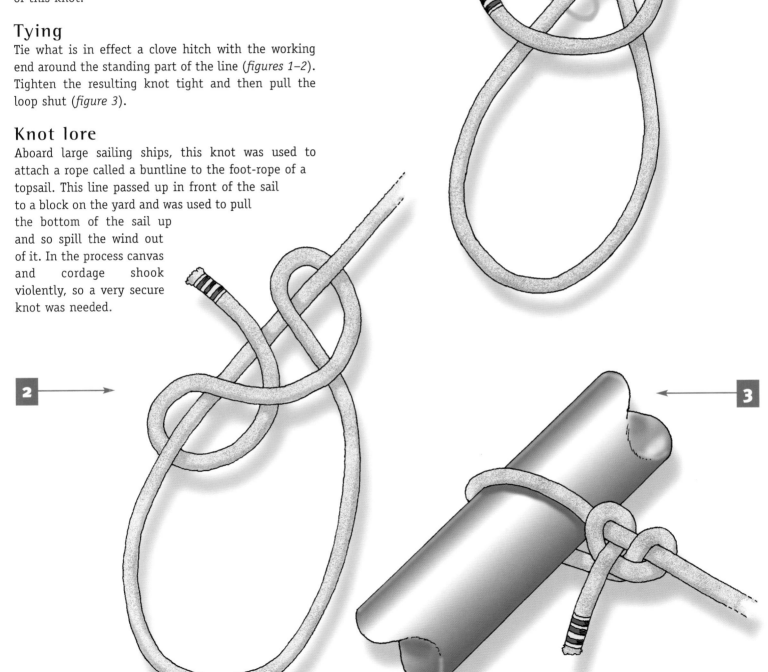

89

ROLLING HITCH

The photograph clearly shows the double knot parts lying on the side of the loaded part of the rope, which goes off the page to the bottom left.

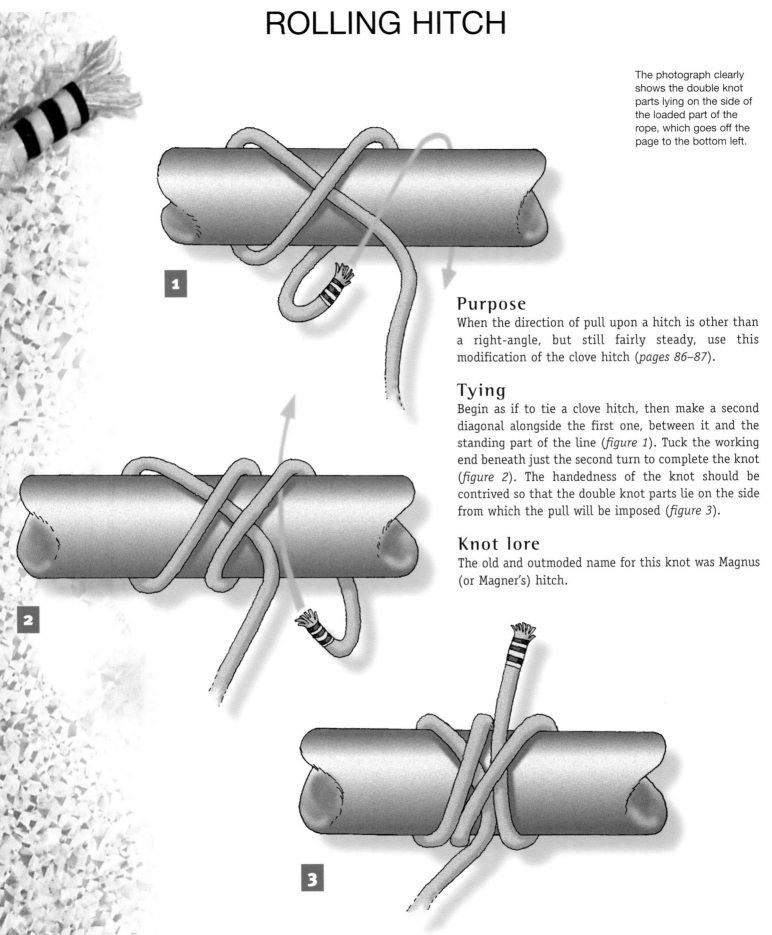

Purpose

When the direction of pull upon a hitch is other than a right-angle, but still fairly steady, use this modification of the clove hitch (*pages 86–87*).

Tying

Begin as if to tie a clove hitch, then make a second diagonal alongside the first one, between it and the standing part of the line (*figure 1*). Tuck the working end beneath just the second turn to complete the knot (*figure 2*). The handedness of the knot should be contrived so that the double knot parts lie on the side from which the pull will be imposed (*figure 3*).

Knot lore

The old and outmoded name for this knot was Magnus (or Magner's) hitch.

MIDSHIPMAN'S HITCH

Purpose

When a slide-and-grip adjustable loop is required, to suspend objects a given height above the ground, or to tension guy-lines, etc., this is the ideal knot.

Tying

Tie what is effectively a rolling hitch (*previous page*) with the working end of the line around its own standing part (*figures 1–3*). Tighten the knot (*figure 4*). By grasping it in the hand, it may be made to slide back and forth to the required position; then, when a load is applied, a dog's leg deformation is created in the standing part of the line, which enables it to hold firm and remain where placed.

Knot lore

The rank of midshipman was that of the most junior officers in the British Royal Navy, unfitted (by virtue of youth and inexperience) for whole-hearted acceptance by either common seamen or other officers, and the target for discrimination by the entire ship's company. Not only does the name of this knot imply a naval origin, therefore, it perhaps hints unfairly at a poor performance.

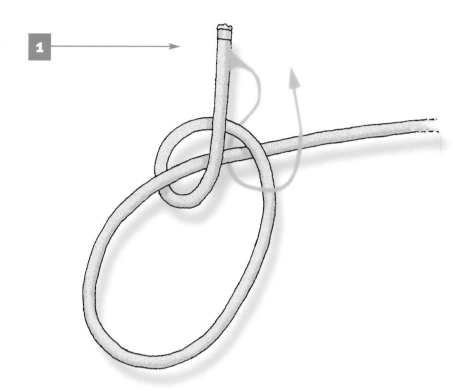

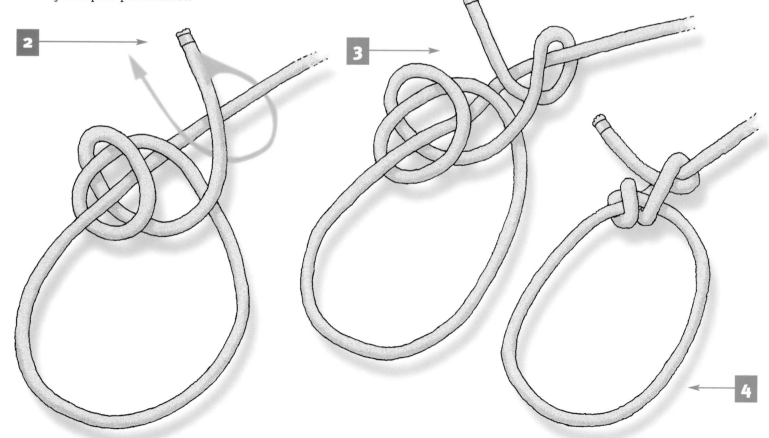

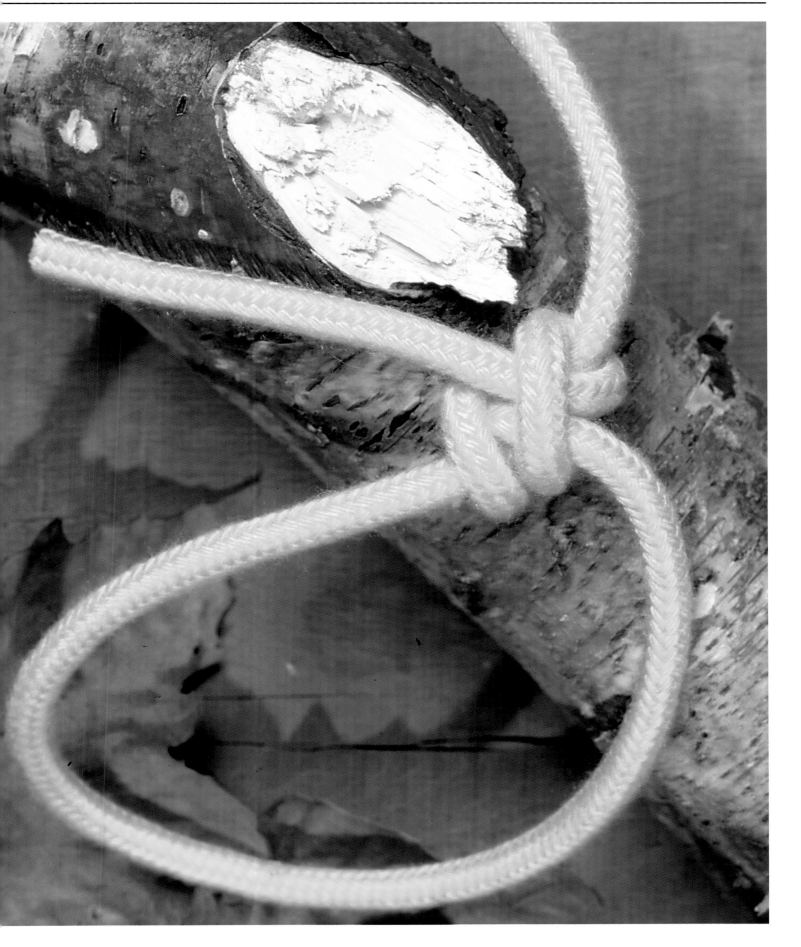

CONSTRICTOR KNOT

Purpose

This is the acme of compact binding knots, an alternative to the strangle knot (*page 48*), with such a tenacious grip that the ends can be trimmed close to the knot without it coming apart.

Tying #1

With a working end, tie a clove hitch (*pages 86–87*), then take an extra tuck to put a half-knot in the two parallel knot parts (*figure 1*). Pull tight (*figure 2*). With tough cord and a solid foundation, such as when seizing a garden hose to an external water source, use a couple of pairs of pliers to exert a powerful force in tightening the knot; or attach a handle to each end (two thick wooden dowels, a pair of screwdrivers, or any else that will improvise a T-shape) with pile hitches. Take care—use gloves or tools—even when tying a batch of these knots hand-tight, since repeated pulling soon rubs raw the creases between finger joints.

A constrictor knot is best removed by cutting it off. With a sharp blade, sever just the diagonal that overlays the entwined knot parts, when the knot will fall away in two curly segments. This way there is little chance of unintentionally marking or scarring whatever the knot was tied around.

Tying #2

To tie in the bight, take a turn and then pull out a bight of the encircling line (*figure 3*). Impart a twist and pass the loop so formed over the end of the foundation on which the knot is being tied (*figures 4–5*).

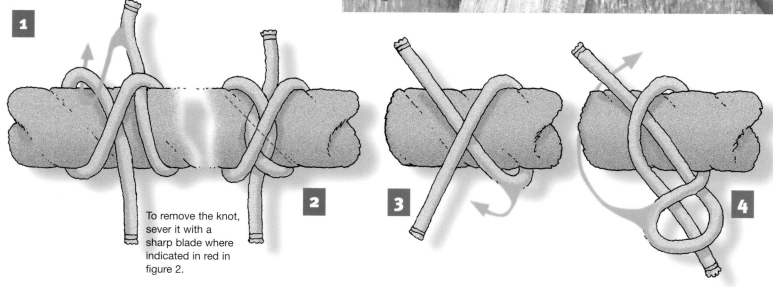

To remove the knot, sever it with a sharp blade where indicated in red in figure 2.

Tying #3

While the constrictor is generally regarded as a semi-permanent seizing that must be cut off when no long required, it may be tied so as to incorporate a quick-release draw-loop (*figures 6–7*).

Knot lore

Clifford Ashley claimed to have discovered this knot for himself some years before he completed *The Ashley Book of Knots* (published in 1944). Unknown to him, however, it had already appeared in a 1931 publication by Finnish Scout leader Martta Ropponen, who knew it as a whip knot, and earlier still in Hjalmar Öhrvall's book *Om Knutar* (1916), where he referred to it as a timber knot. Lester Copestake, a member of the International Guild of Knot Tyers, believes it is also the gunner's knot, used to seize the necks of the flannel bags of gunpowder that acted as cartridges in muzzle loading field guns, described—but frustratingly not illustrated—in *The Book of Knots* (1890) by Tom Bowling. Then again, the scholarly Cyrus Lawrence Day points out, in *Quipus & Witches' Knots* (University of Kansas Press, 1967), that this knot may be identical with one described—but again not illustrated—by the Ancient Greek physician Herakles in the first century AD for use as a surgical sling. There is evidently not much that is truly new in knotting.

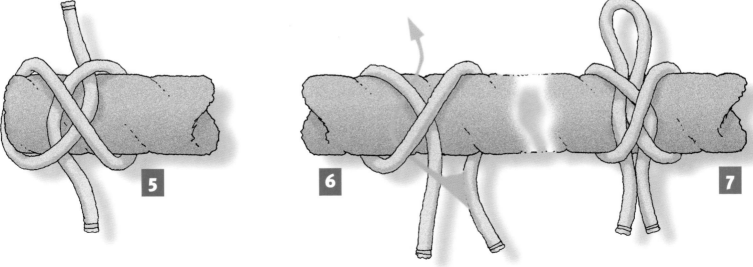

DOUBLE CONSTRICTOR KNOT

Purpose

The basic constrictor knot depends for its security on the diagonal knot part lying firmly across the entwined knot parts beneath it, like a helping finger on a half-completed shoe lace tie. When the diameter of whatever is being bound is large, the basic knot is less effective. The remedy is a double constrictor knot.

Tying #1

Begin as for a rolling hitch but then tuck the working end as shown (*figure 1*). Tighten the knot (*figure 2*).

Tying #2

When the end of the foundation is accessible, it is possible to tie this knot in the bight. First make a clove hitch (in the bight) and rearrange it by moving the upper end to the extreme left (*figures 3–4*). Pull out a bight, impart half a twist and slip it over the end of the foundation (*figures 5–6*).

Knot lore

The method of tying a double constrictor knot in the bight first appeared in *Knots* (1990) by US master rigger Brion Toss, a member of the International Guild of Knot Tyers.

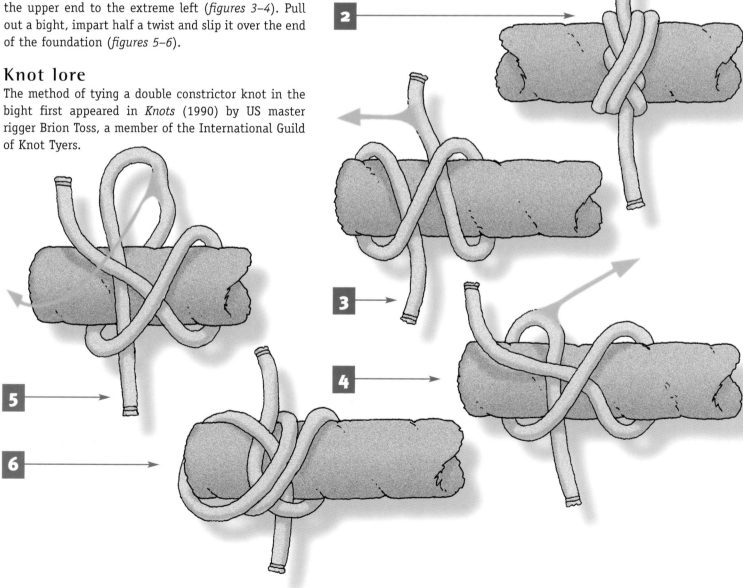

TRANSOM KNOT

Purpose

To seize two cross-pieces of wood, when assembling the framework for a kite or a garden trellis, use this binding knot. It resembles a constrictor knot (which is why it is included in this section) but is in fact a modified double overhand or strangle knot.

Tying

Wrap, interweave and tuck with a working end as shown (*figures 1–2*).

Knot lore

This neat knot was discovered and published by Clifford Ashley in his *Book of Knots* (1944).

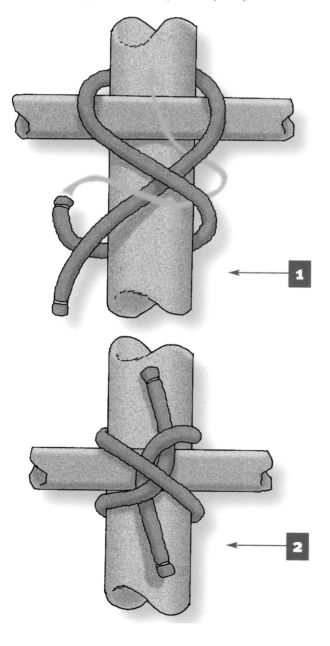

GROUND LINE HITCH COIL

Purpose
Here is yet another method of securing a coil of rope to be carried or hung up.

Tying
Coil the rope as usual, then form a bight in the working end and tie the knot known as a ground line hitch with this doubled end as shown (*figures 1–2*).

SNUGGLE HITCH

Purpose

When a clove hitch (*pages 86–87*) is not sufficient for the job in hand, the gentle curves and frictional crossovers of this hitch make it a stronger and more secure alternative. It will cope with a pull at right-angles to the rail, spar, or whatever else forms the point of attachment, and will withstand a pull or load that varies in direction and strength.

Tying

Begin as if to tie a clove hitch, but then divert the working end to wrap and tuck as shown (*figures 1–3*). Pull the knot snug and tight (*figure 4*). For a lengthwise pull, locate the two parallel wrapping turns on the side of the loaded standing part as the direction of pull.

Knot lore

This comparative newcomer to the knotting scene was devised by Yorkshireman Owen K. Nuttall, a member of the International Guild of Knot Tyers, and published in the Guild's quarterly magazine *Knotting Matters* (in January 1987).

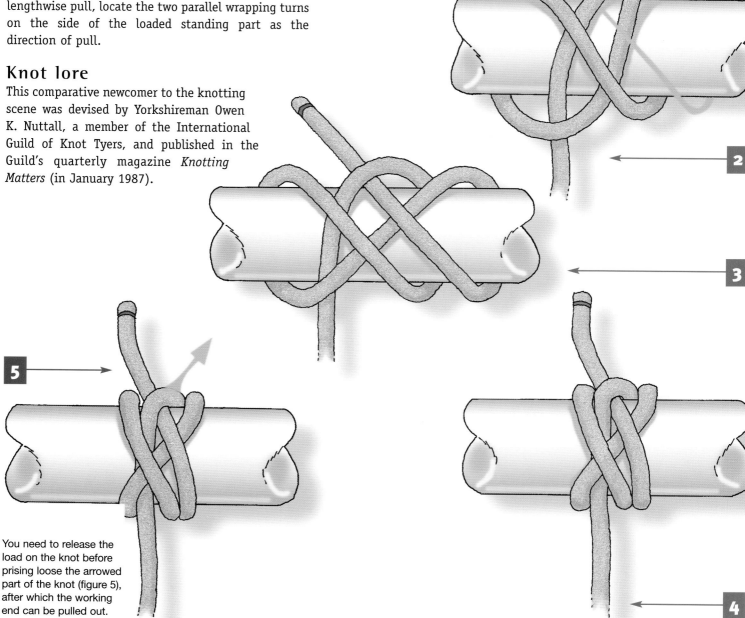

You need to release the load on the knot before prising loose the arrowed part of the knot (figure 5), after which the working end can be pulled out.

DOUBLE FIGURE OF EIGHT HITCH

Purpose
Use this as a tougher alternative to the constrictor (*pages 94–95*) and strangle knots (*page 48*) for demanding work that might prove too much for even those two stalwart bindings.

Tying
Lay down a couple of alternate loops, then place another pair on top of the first (*figures 1–2*). Insert the foundation as indicated, pick it up and turn it over, then arrange and tighten the knot (*figure 3*).

Knot lore
Owen K. Nuttall, a member of the International Guild of Knot Tyers, encountered this knot on his way to discovering the snuggle hitch (previously described), but, it seems to me, that it makes a better binding knot.

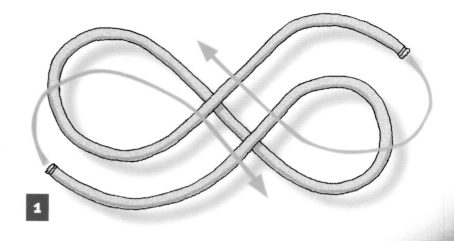

1

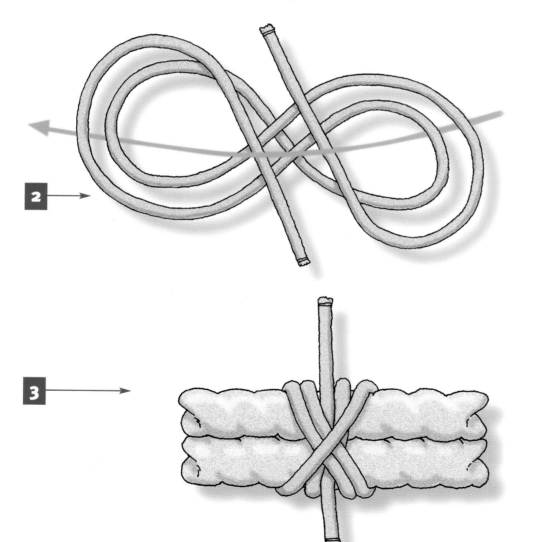

2

3

BOOM HITCH

Purpose
Use this heavy-duty shire horse of a hitch instead of the snuggle hitch (*pages 100–101*) when the direction and strength of load is highly variable.

Tying
Begin as if to tie a ground line hitch but then wrap over-over-over and finally tuck as shown (*figures 1–3*).

Knot lore
Clifford Ashley seems to have been the first to described this hitch in the *Ashley Book of Knots* (1944).

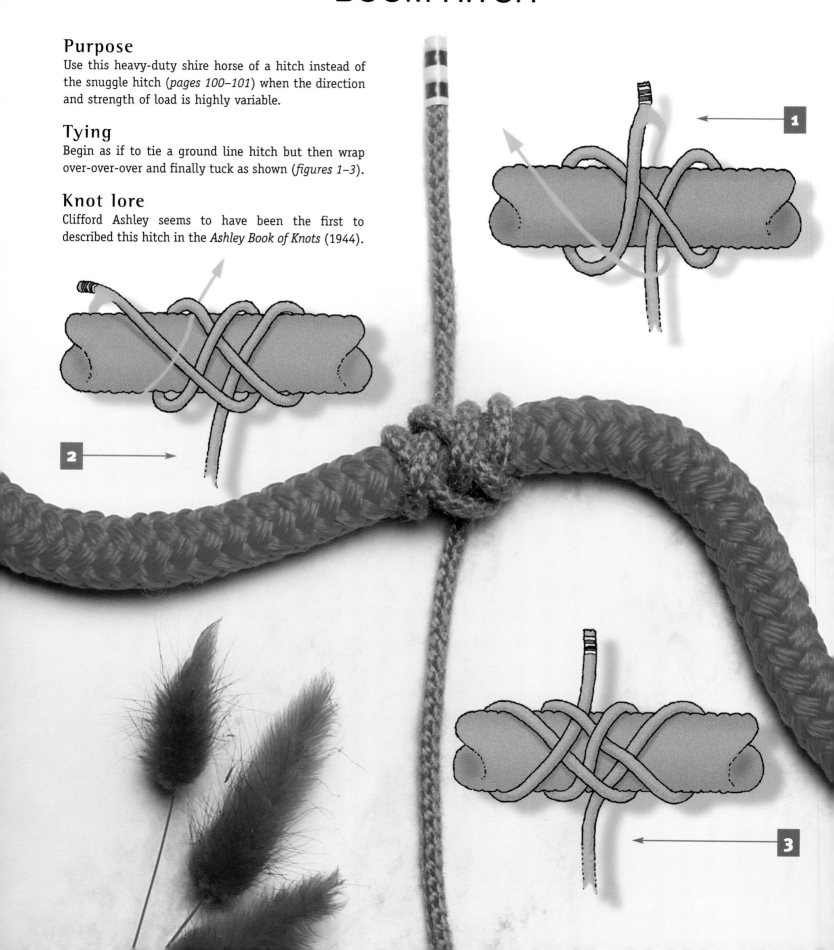

SECTION 5
OTHER USEFUL KNOTS

The study of knots is...endless.
(Heather McLeay—*The Knots Puzzle Book*, 1994)

The selection of knots that follows has been chosen
to challenge and inspire all who are keen to add more
knots to their repertoire. Some, such as the carrick
bend, are straightforward working knots. Others, like
the braid knot and the square knot, are just as
practical but add a touch of decoration wherever they
are tied; for, while all knots have their uses, many
happen to be ornamental too. A few (including the
frustrator and the Lapp knot) are either new or
virtually unknown, while the Chinese cloverleaf and
the T-shaped Turk's head are isolated representatives
of large and complex knot families.

COMMON WHIPPING

Purpose

This quick and easy whipping should be applied to the unseized end of any rope or other sizeable bit of cordage that would otherwise unravel and fray. Synthetic hawser-laid ropes by their very nature lack cohesion and must be heat-sealed, taped or whipped. This particular whipping's weakness is its simplicity. It will, as a consequence, come adrift if subjected to rough treatment; and, if even a single turn snaps, the entire whipping unwinds.

More robust alternatives to this whipping are either the West Country whipping (*pages 42–43*) or a 5-lead x 4-bight Turk's head (*pages 150–151*). Still this is a useful first aid treatment with which to bandage cut ropes.

Tying

It can be helpful to whip toward the cut end and in the opposite direction to the lay of the rope, for the most effective result. Tight binding tends to open up the lay, which (as it springs back) tightens the whipping. First lay a bight or loop along the line, then wrap the working end to enclose it (*figures 1–2*).

Tuck the working end of the whipping twine down through the remaining bit of bight and pull on the other end to trap it (*figure 3*). Continue to pull, so that it is dragged beneath the wrapping turns of the whipping, until the resulting interlocked elbows lie in the middle (*figure 4*).

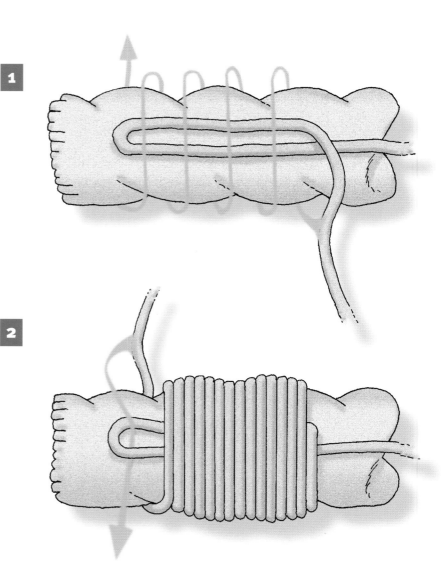

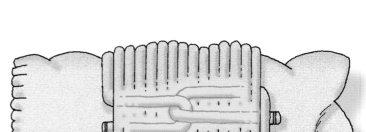

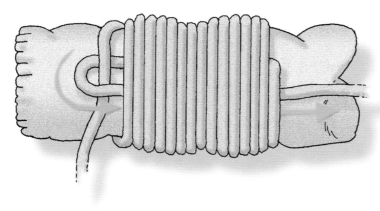

TIMBER & KILLICK HITCHES

Purpose

These two forms of the same basic knot are intended to haul or hoist logs or entire tree trunks. They will also drag or tow wooden piling, lengths of conduit pipe or any other similar objects.

Tying

Take the working end once around the standing part of the rope and improvise a running eye by wrapping (dogging) the end several times around itself. Pull tight and a timber hitch results (*figure 1*). To ensure the load drags or tows in a straight line, add one (or more) half hitches some distance from the initial knot. This is a killick hitch (*figure 2*).

Knot lore

The timber hitch was mentioned in *A Treatise on Rigging* (c.1625) and was illustrated in the *Encyclopédie* (1762) of Denis Diderot. It is an old knot. A killick was the naval term for a small anchor, and for any odd weight (such as a lump of stone) that might be employed on the end of a line (secured by a killick hitch) to anchor a dinghy, buoy or fisherman's lobster pot to the sea-bed. The killick hitch was named and illustrated in *Elements and Practice of Rigging and Seamanship* (1794) by David Steel.

1 →

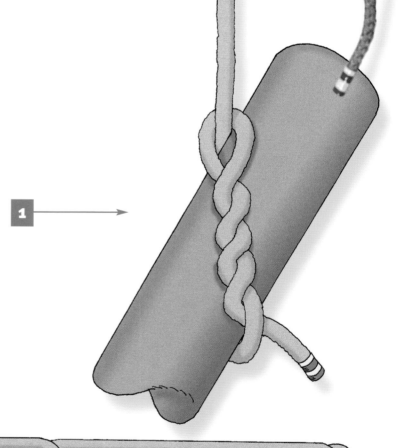

2 →

ALPINE BUTTERFLY KNOT

Purpose
This delightfully named knot is intended to form a fixed loop in the standing part of a rope used as a safety line or tether, to which a person or item of equipment may then be clipped. It will withstand a pull from any direction.

Tying
It is quickly tied in the bight as shown (*figures 1–2*) but must then be worked carefully into shape before it is tightened (*figure 3*).

Knot lore
With a background spent in European mountaineering resorts, this is a classy old dame. "If the bowline is the King of Knots, this must surely be the Queen," wrote John Sweet in his book *Scout Pioneering* (1974).

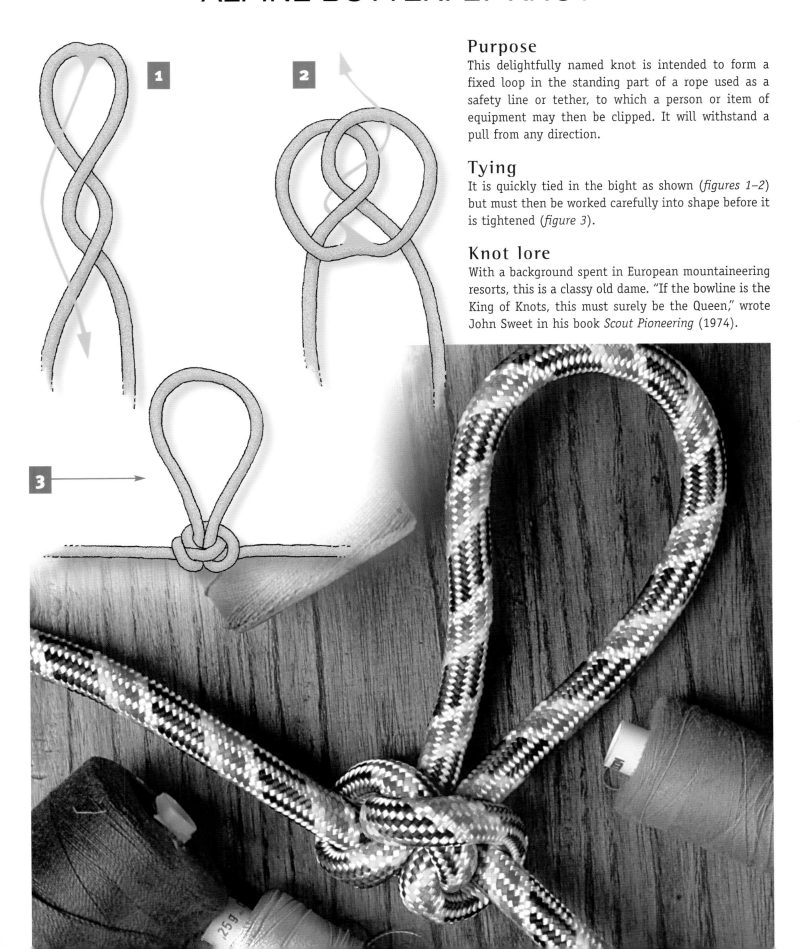

REEF (or SQUARE) KNOT LOOP

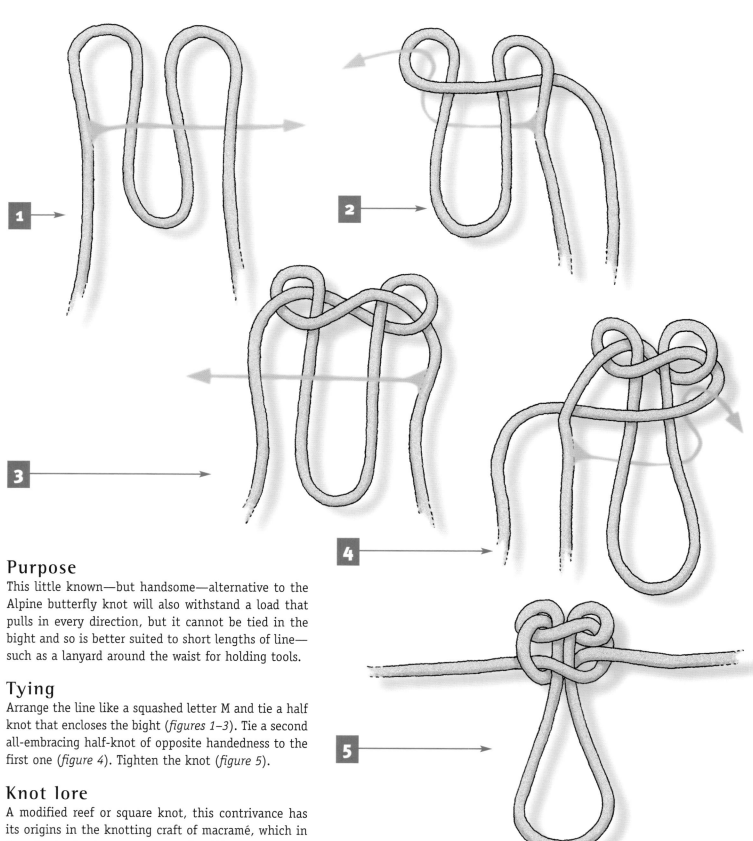

Purpose

This little known—but handsome—alternative to the Alpine butterfly knot will also withstand a load that pulls in every direction, but it cannot be tied in the bight and so is better suited to short lengths of line—such as a lanyard around the waist for holding tools.

Tying

Arrange the line like a squashed letter M and tie a half knot that encloses the bight (*figures 1–3*). Tie a second all-embracing half-knot of opposite handedness to the first one (*figure 4*). Tighten the knot (*figure 5*).

Knot lore

A modified reef or square knot, this contrivance has its origins in the knotting craft of macramé, which in America is also known as square-knotting.

THE FRUSTRATOR

Purpose
This wholly unknown knot is a binding knot at least as effective as the constrictor in all respects.

Tying #1
Using a working end, wrap and tuck as shown (*figures 1–2*). Tighten by tugging on both ends, but particularly the working end which exerts an almost ratchet-like grip upon the turns of this knot (*figure 3*).

Tying #2
The fact that this knot, when slid off the end of its foundation, falls apart and vanishes means that it can also be tied in the bight (*figures 4–6*).

1 ⟶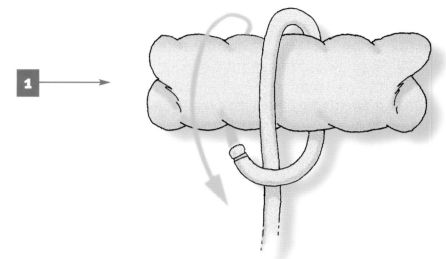

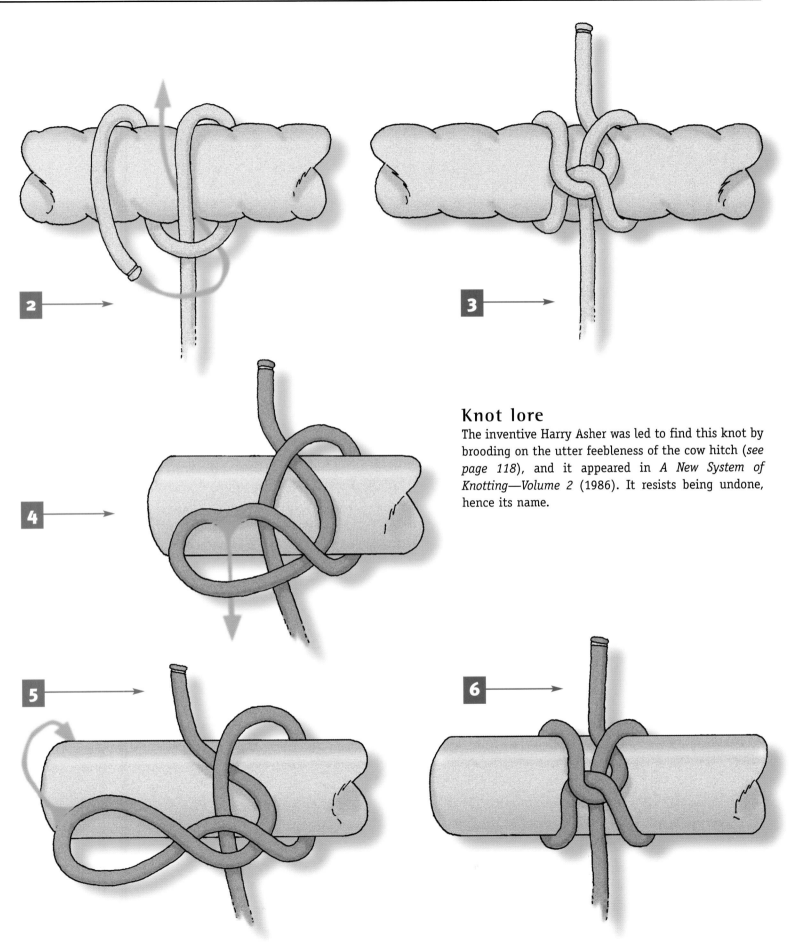

Knot lore

The inventive Harry Asher was led to find this knot by brooding on the utter feebleness of the cow hitch (*see page 118*), and it appeared in *A New System of Knotting—Volume 2* (1986). It resists being undone, hence its name.

HIGHWAYMAN'S HITCH

Purpose

This makes a handy hitch for light loads when quick-release may be needed. It is not suited to heavy work as, in some cordage, it can capsize and spill. Tied in the middle of a line, the working end may be tugged (to release the draw-loop and free the knot) from a distance.

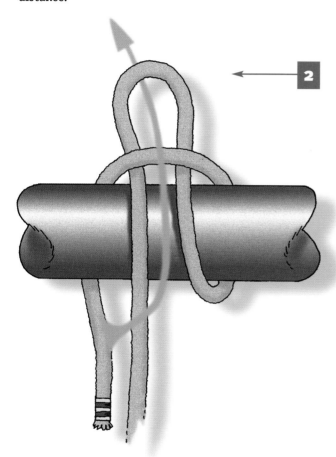

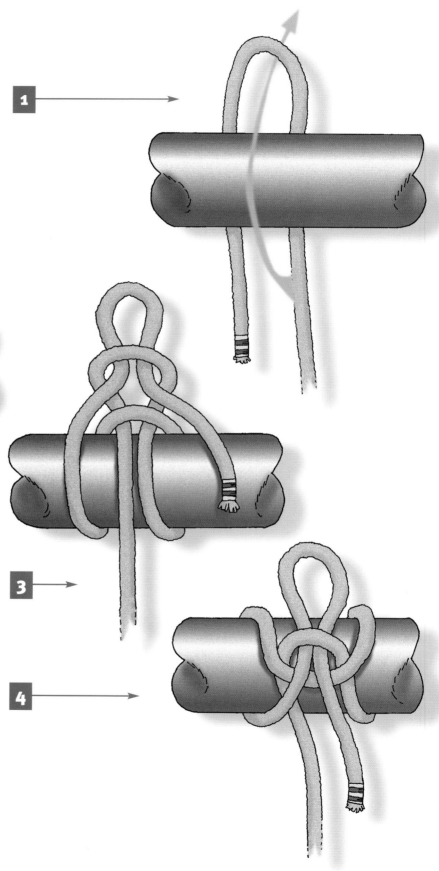

Tying

Build up this hitch from one draw-loop slipped inside another draw-loop (*figures 1–3*). Tighten carefully (*figure 4*).

Knot lore

There is no evidence that this knot was ever used by highwaymen; but children who learn the knot—more as a trick than for any practical purpose (enjoying the way its apparent complexity melts away with one pull on the working end)—like to believe that was how it acquired its name.

PILE, POST or STAKE HITCH

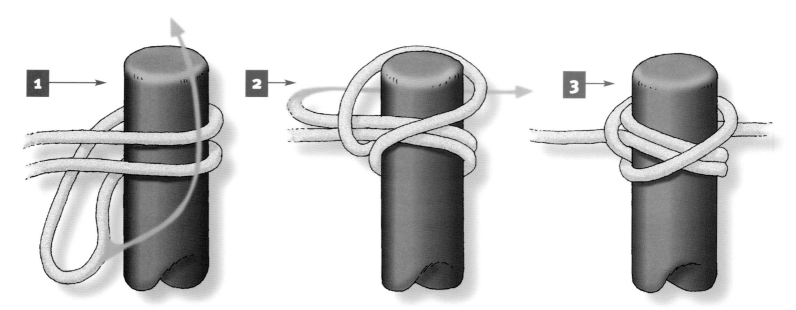

Purpose

As the name implies, this is a means of attaching a barrier rope or plastic tape to a series of uprights, whether at road works, a country fair or a crime scene. It can also be modified for use in fixing the end of a cord to an improvised handle to gain extra purchase in pulling tight constrictor, frustrator and strangle knots.

Tying #1

Tie it in the bight by the simple expedient of wrapping the doubled line around the anchorage point, and then looping it beneath the standing part to go over the top of the pile, post or stake (*figures 1–2*). The two lengths of line will then usually be led off in opposite directions (*figure 3*).

Tying #2

When attaching the end of a cord to an improvised handle, such as a screwdriver, or other implement (*see right*), arrange it so that the loaded end is furthest away from the retaining bight. This way it is quite secure; otherwise it is considerably less so.

Knot lore

When, some years ago, the editor of *Knotting Matters*—the quarterly magazine of the International Guild of Knot Tyers—asked readers which knot (if only one was allowed) they would like to see taught, the insightful John Smith, of the Surrey Branch in England, proposed this knot. It could, he demonstrated, be adapted for use as a knot, bend or hitch in every imaginable situation.

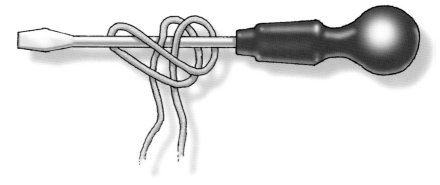

PEDIGREE COW HITCH

Purpose

A lightweight attachment, scorned by many knot tyers, the common cow hitch is insecure since any load falls on only the standing part. It can be tied quickly and easily by several methods, however, which makes it handy for starting lashings or suspending items in a garage, outdoor storage area, office or studio. If it is to be used, then this adaptation of the basic hitch is recommended.

Tying #1

Flop a bight over the beam, spar or rail and pull both ends of the cord or lanyard through as shown (*figures 1–2*). This results in the common and despised cow hitch. Tuck the working end (*figure 3*) to convert it into a pedigree version.

Tying #2

Alternatively, the knot may be tied directly with the working end (*figure 4*).

Tying #3

The basic knot can also be tied in the bight and then slipped over the end of its anchorage point (*figures 5–6*), then the final tuck made.

Knot lore

Harry Asher first published this simple knot in *The Alternative Knot Book* (1989) and it was shortly afterwards adopted by the Girl Guides Association for Level One of their Knotter's Badge.

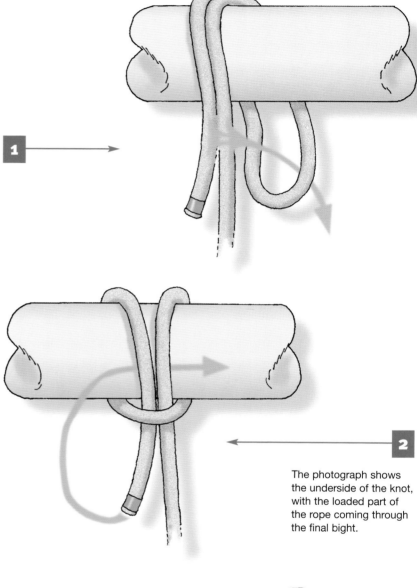

The photograph shows the underside of the knot, with the loaded part of the rope coming through the final bight.

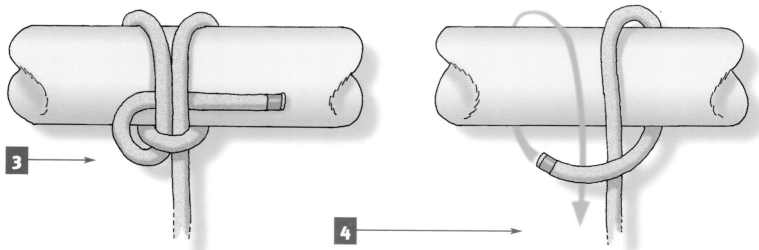

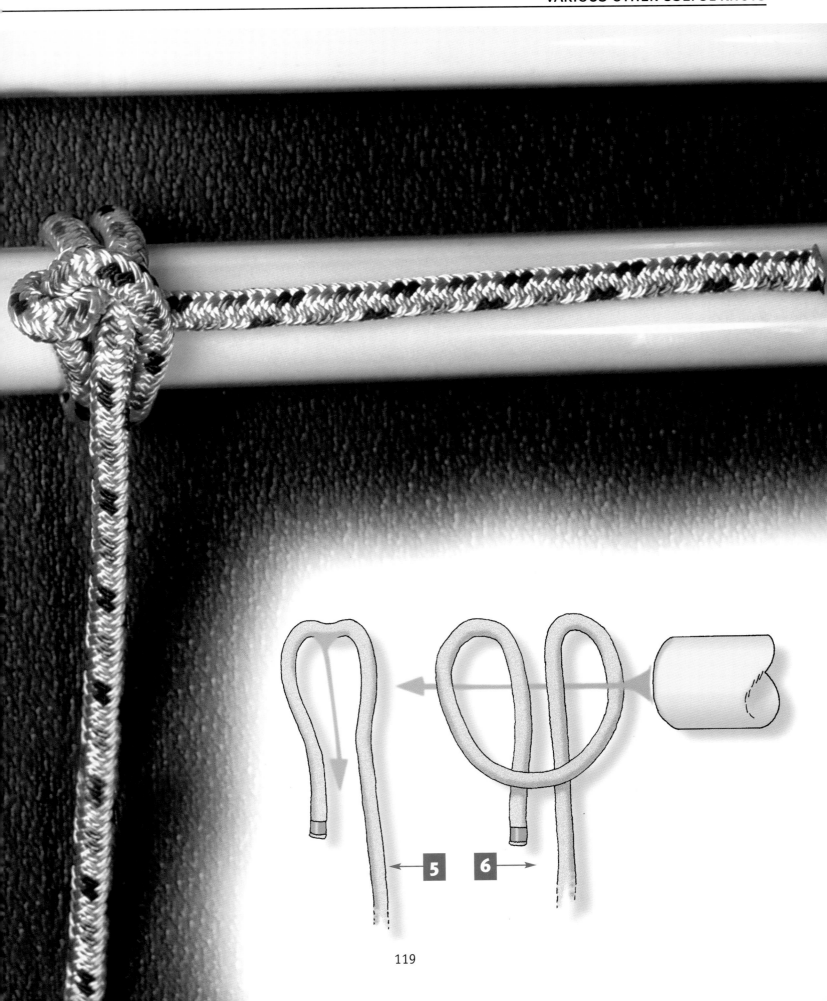

BULL HITCH

Purpose
This is an alternative to the pedigree cow hitch (*previous page*) which, like that knot, may be tied either directly (with an end) or in the bight.

Tying #1
Bend a bight into a pair of loops, one slightly larger than the other (*figure 1*). Wrap the larger of the two loops in a 360° circuit, going over and around the smaller loop (*figure 2*). Slip the resulting knot onto its foundation and tighten (*figure 3*).

Tying #2
When a ring or rail without an available end is the point of attachment, tie this knot directly with a working end (*figures 4–6*).

Knot lore
This modified version of a cow hitch was reported by Robert Pont (a member of the International Guild of Knot Tyers) in *Knotting Matters* (January 1995). He called it the Piwich knot, after a child named Piwich Kust of the Bois Brule tribe whom he had seen tie it in Quebec, Canada. As it is a beefed-up and stronger version of a cow hitch it was too tempting not to rename it a bull hitch.

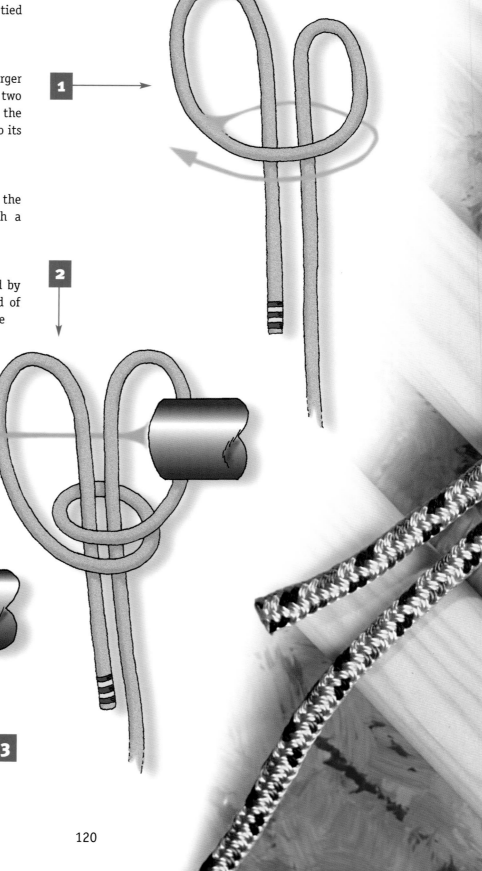

PRUSIK KNOT

Purpose

This is another of those slide-and-grip knots that may be grasped in the hand and shifted to the required position, after which—around a foundation with any sort of friction at all, such as rough wood or a rope with a matt finish—it may be loaded. It will withstand a pull from varying directions.

Tying

Begin as if tying a common cow hitch (*figures 1–2*) then pull out the working bight and wrap and tuck it a second time (*figure 3*). Tighten the knot (*figure 4*).

Knot lore

Austrian professor of music Karl Prusik devised this knot during the First World War to mend broken strings on musical instruments. Later, in 1931, he popularized its use in mountaineering. A variety of such slide-and-grip knots or hitches now exist and they are collectively known as prusiking knots (with a small "p").

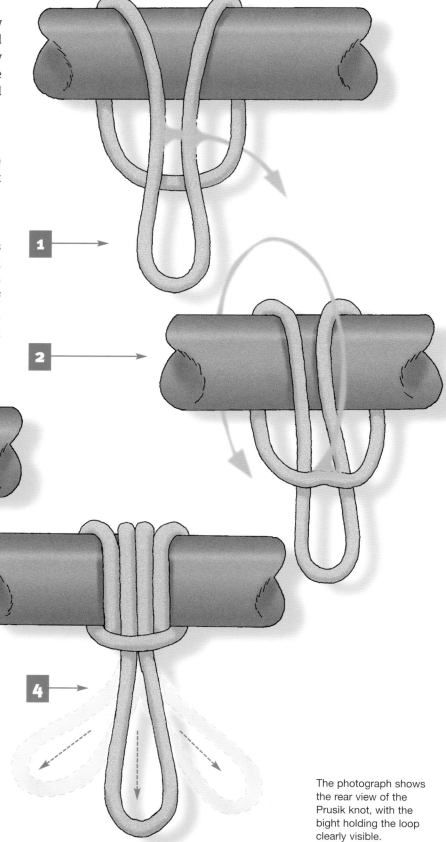

The loop in figure 4 may be loaded in either direction.

The photograph shows the rear view of the Prusik knot, with the bight holding the loop clearly visible.

ASHER'S BOTTLE SLING

Purpose

Bottles of liquid—whether containing plant fertilizer, battery topping-up fluid or one's most-loved beverage—can be heavy and sometimes slippery. This is one of a number of sling knots that exists to grip the necks of glass and earthenware in such a way that bottles and other containers may be carried comfortably or hung up out of harm's way.

Tying

Begin as if to tie a Prusik knot (*previous page*), then impart a half-twist in the upper bight and tuck the other bight through it (*figure 1*). Pull the second bight down (*figure 2*) and painstakingly tighten the entire arrangement (*figure 3*).

Knot lore

This is—as its name implies—yet another ingenious contrivance from the inventive fingers of Harry Asher, that first appeared in *A New System of Knotting— Volume 2* (1989).

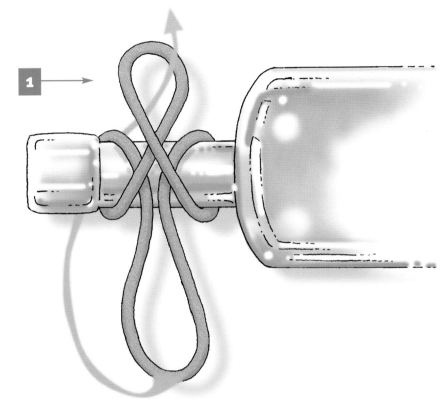

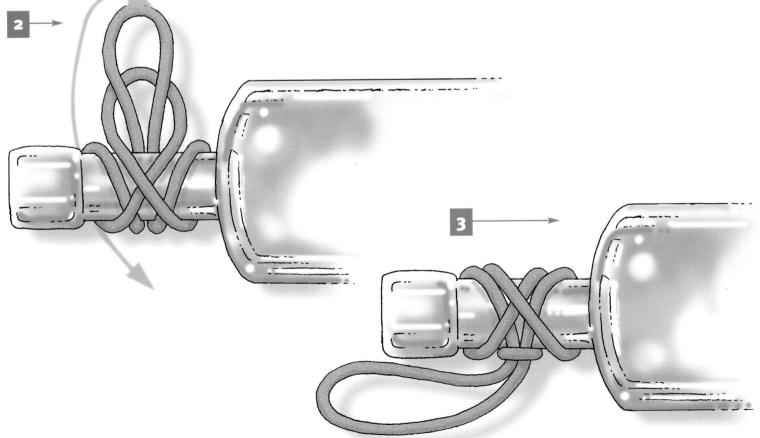

JUG, JAR or BOTTLE SLING

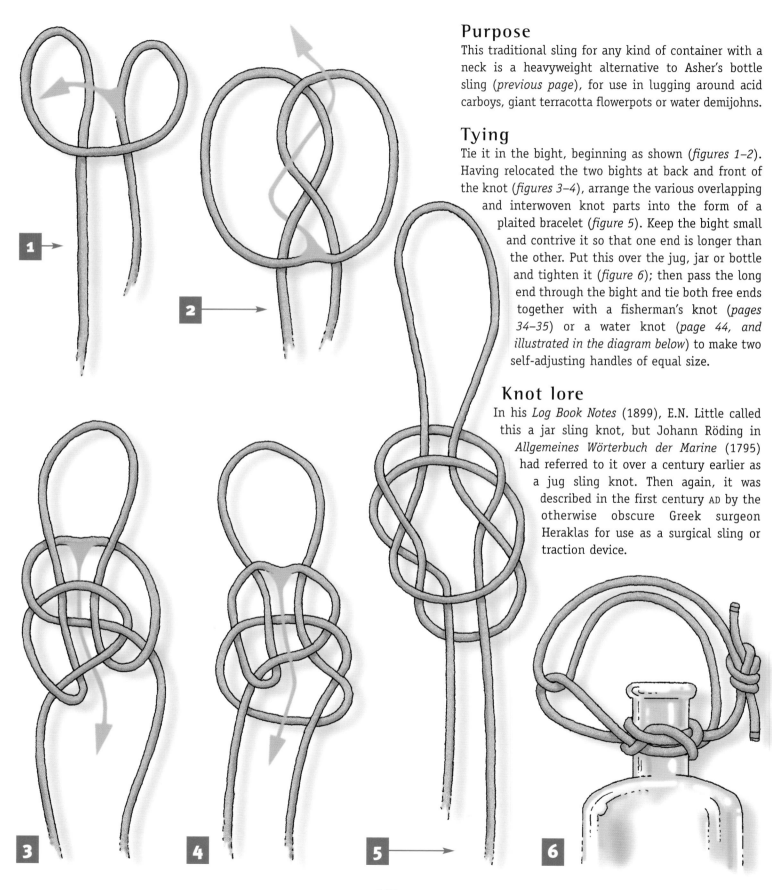

Purpose

This traditional sling for any kind of container with a neck is a heavyweight alternative to Asher's bottle sling (*previous page*), for use in lugging around acid carboys, giant terracotta flowerpots or water demijohns.

Tying

Tie it in the bight, beginning as shown (*figures 1–2*). Having relocated the two bights at back and front of the knot (*figures 3–4*), arrange the various overlapping and interwoven knot parts into the form of a plaited bracelet (*figure 5*). Keep the bight small and contrive it so that one end is longer than the other. Put this over the jug, jar or bottle and tighten it (*figure 6*); then pass the long end through the bight and tie both free ends together with a fisherman's knot (*pages 34–35*) or a water knot (*page 44, and illustrated in the diagram below*) to make two self-adjusting handles of equal size.

Knot lore

In his *Log Book Notes* (1899), E.N. Little called this a jar sling knot, but Johann Röding in *Allgemeines Wörterbuch der Marine* (1795) had referred to it over a century earlier as a jug sling knot. Then again, it was described in the first century AD by the otherwise obscure Greek surgeon Heraklas for use as a surgical sling or traction device.

BRAID KNOT

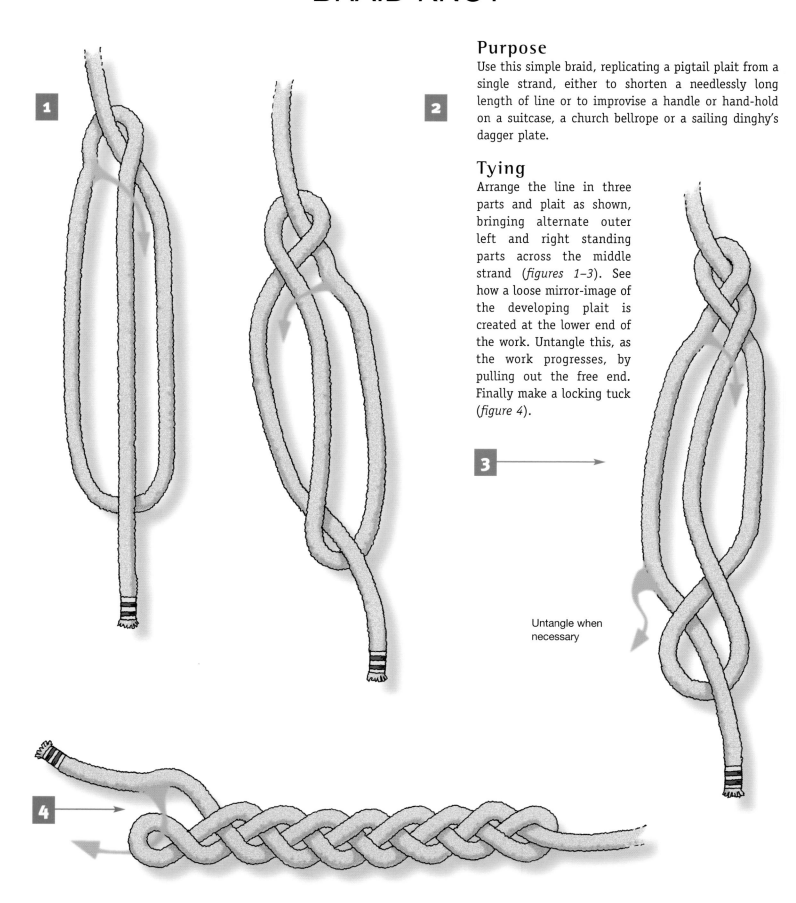

Purpose
Use this simple braid, replicating a pigtail plait from a single strand, either to shorten a needlessly long length of line or to improvise a handle or hand-hold on a suitcase, a church bellrope or a sailing dinghy's dagger plate.

Tying
Arrange the line in three parts and plait as shown, bringing alternate outer left and right standing parts across the middle strand (*figures 1–3*). See how a loose mirror-image of the developing plait is created at the lower end of the work. Untangle this, as the work progresses, by pulling out the free end. Finally make a locking tuck (*figure 4*).

Untangle when necessary

SQUARE KNOT

Purpose

Perhaps the best of all uses for this knot is to tie a neck-scarf beneath one's chin. The good-looking four-part crown neatly fills the open V-neck of a blouse or shirt, while at the same time ensuring that the each free end hangs down at a chic angle.

Tying

Each end in turn is used to create this knot (*figures 1–3*). The finished form is distinctive, with a good-looking front side that is displayed and a nondescript rear face to be concealed (*figures 4–5*).

Knot lore

Those who refer to the reef knot as a square knot need another name for this one, and rustler's knot is as good as any.

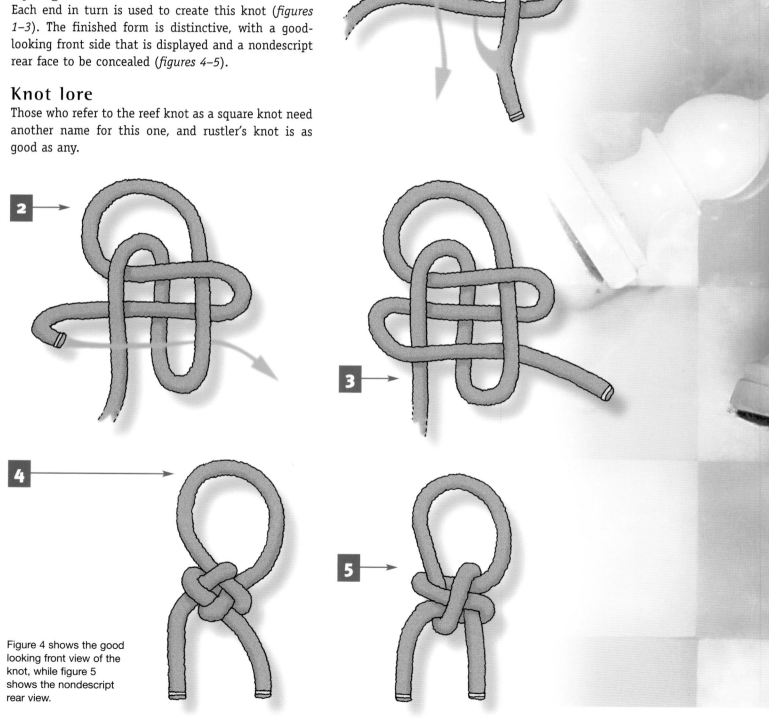

Figure 4 shows the good looking front view of the knot, while figure 5 shows the nondescript rear view.

130

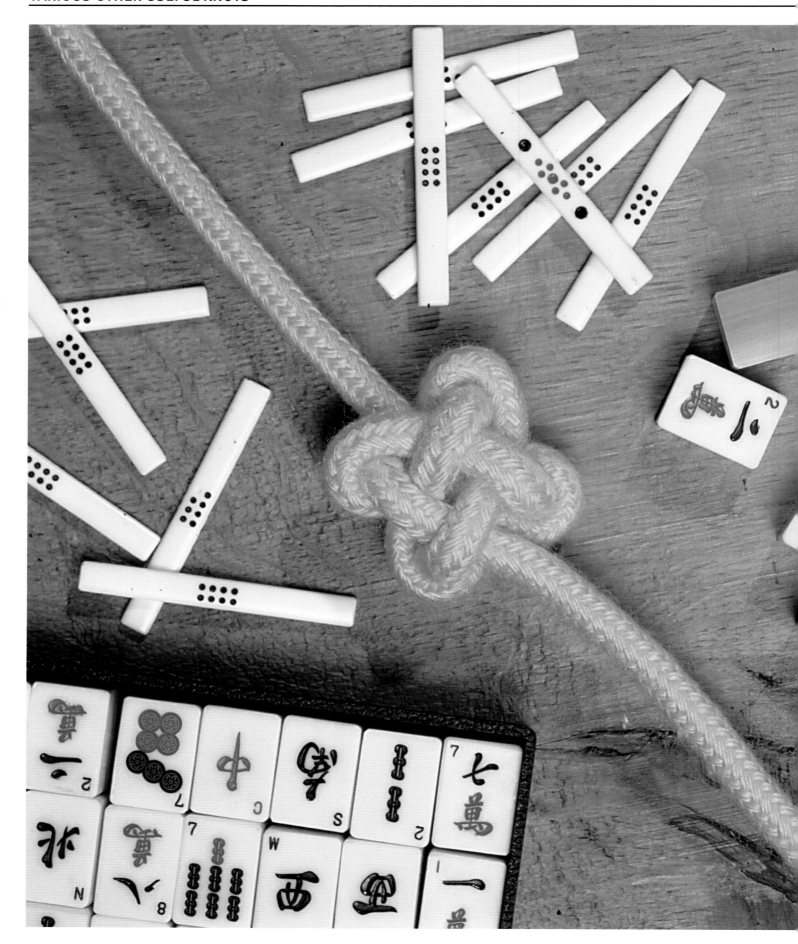

CHINESE CLOVERLEAF

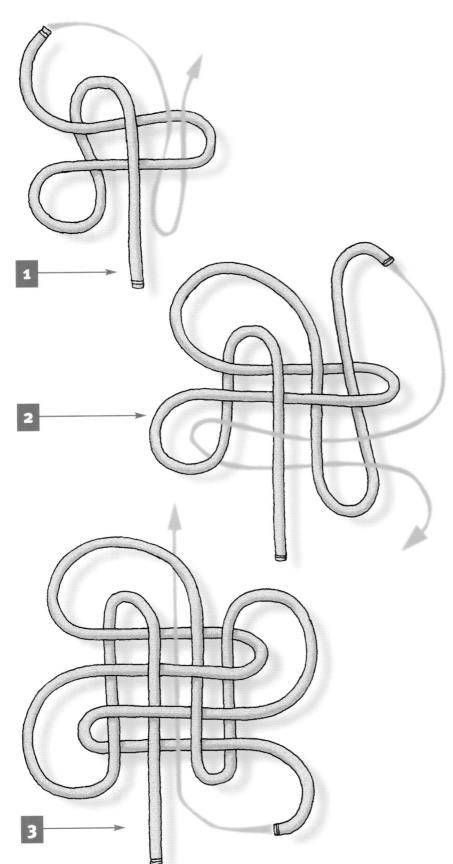

Purpose

This unusual knot will embellish a single-cord lanyard (from light pull to medium tug) or a dressing gown waist-tie—even the retaining cord on a monocle for the rare eccentric who still sports such an eye-glass. Use it, too, as ornamentation on gift packages.

Tying

A pin-board and some pins are often recommended to secure the layout of this knot in its early stages, before the final locking tuck is inserted; but with a confident mind (and a discerning eye) it can be done readily enough in the hand without such paraphernalia. The knot consists of four interlocked bights (*figures 1–3*), which are then drawn snug to form a four-part crown knot enhanced by quadruple corner rim parts (*figure 4*). Both faces (front and rear) are identical.

Knot lore

This is one of a large family of more elaborate Chinese knots that may be thousands of years old. The tradition attaching to it is the same as in the West, that any cloverleaf is lucky (and a four-part one more so).

MATTHEW WALKER KNOT

Purpose

This is a gathering knot, to hold neatly any two matching strands that enter the knot together and emerge at the opposite end still together. As such it is a practical yet ornamental embellishment to any lanyard.

Tying

Begin as shown (*figure 1*) and tie a half-knot to enclose both standing parts (*figures 2–3*). Take each working end in turn across the knot (forward facing one in front, rear facing one behind) and tuck it through its own loop (*figures 3–5*). Tighten gradually, with an even tension on all parts, allowing the two standing parts to swap sides (*figure 6*). All Matthew Walkers, of which this is but the simplest, are essentially an assembly of strands, each of which is tied in an overhand knot.

Knot lore

Prior to the 20th century this knot seems to have been the only one named after a person. Nobody knows who Matthew Walker was, although it is often suggested that he might have been a rigger in one of the British Royal Naval dockyards. Other knots named after people now include Ashley's stopper knot, Hunter's bend, and Asher's bottle sling, quite apart from the numerous personalized knots employed by climbers and anglers.

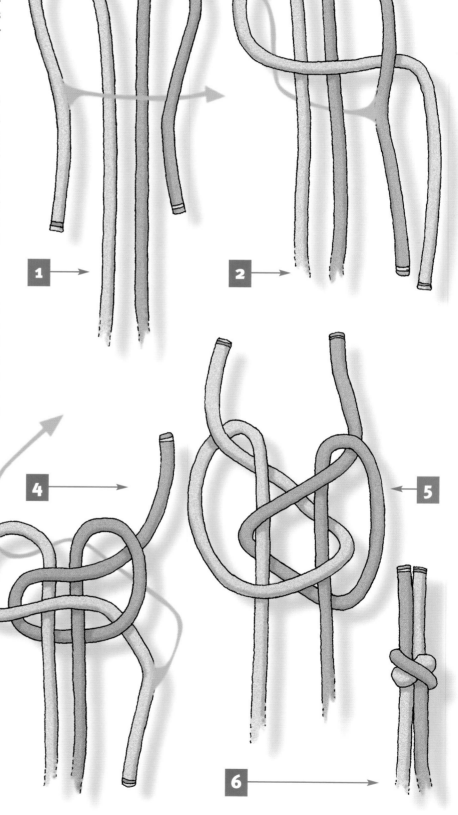

CHINESE LANYARD KNOT

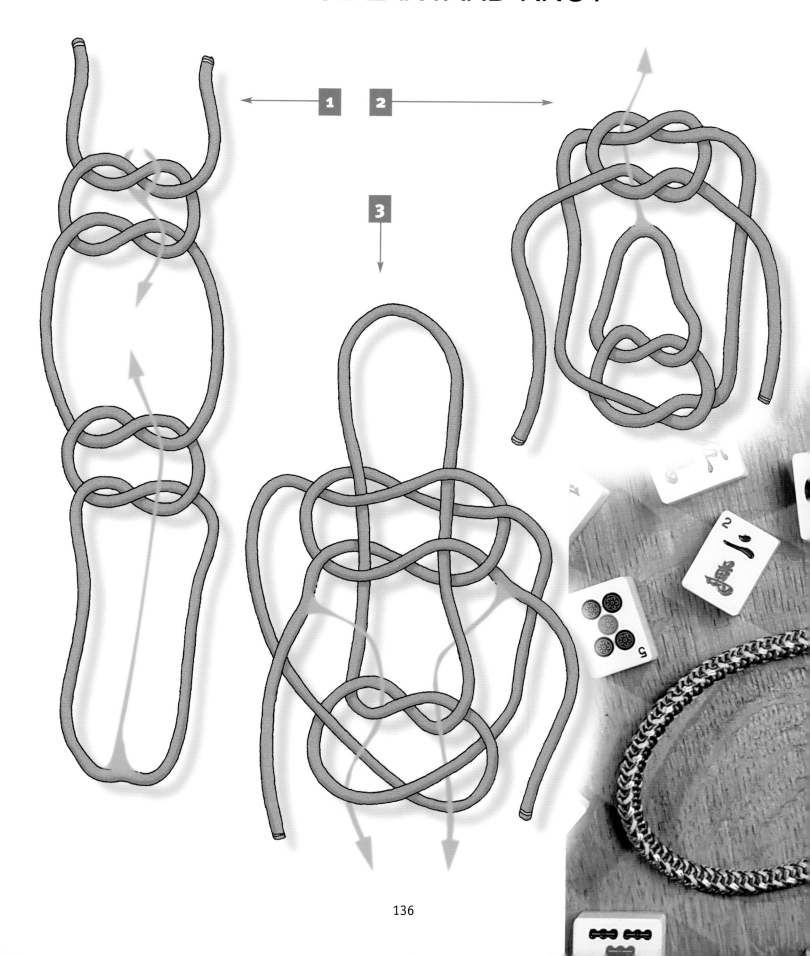

Purpose

This singular knot can be worn and shown off as a string neck-tie or amulet; but it is also one of those knots that are tied for the simple satisfaction of demonstrating that one can do it.

Tying

In a doubled length of line first tie two matching pairs of half-knots, or two granny knots, all of identical handedness (*figure 1*). Invert both granny knots, turning them in toward one another (*figure 2*). Pull the closed bight through the twin upper half-knots to protrude like a tongue from between their twisted lips; and then tuck the free ends in turn (front and back) down through the lower pair of half-knots (*figure 3*).

Tighten this knot with the utmost patience, since a careless and rushed approach will distort it beyond recognition and render it impossible to achieve the final shape. Concentrate first on creating the central four-part crown knot (*figure 4*). Next tighten top and bottom half-knots (*figure 5*). Finally work the slack from each of the projecting lateral bights, losing it either in the loop or the free ends, until the final form is inevitable (*figure 6*).

Knot lore

The highly decorated ceilings (plafonds) of Chinese temples and palaces traditionally used this pattern as an ornamental motif, which is why the knotting writer Lydia Chen calls it the plafond knot.

VICE VERSA

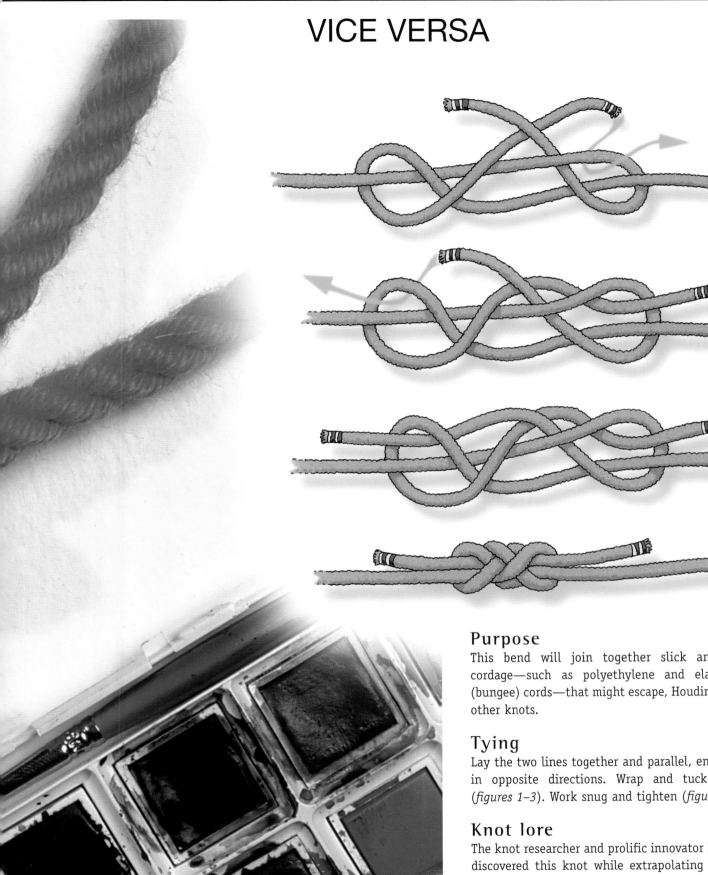

Purpose

This bend will join together slick and slippery cordage—such as polyethylene and elastic shock (bungee) cords—that might escape, Houdini-like, from other knots.

Tying

Lay the two lines together and parallel, ends pointing in opposite directions. Wrap and tuck as shown (*figures 1–3*). Work snug and tighten (*figure 4*).

Knot lore

The knot researcher and prolific innovator Harry Asher discovered this knot while extrapolating all possible permutations of the common sheet bend. It first appeared in *A New System of Knotting* (1986) and was later published in *The Alternative Knot Book* (1989).

LAPP KNOT

Purpose

Many knots that incorporate a draw-loop as a means of quick-release may still not come apart completely. This is especially true of waist-ties, when bodily pressure and friction between working end and loop can still require hands to pull the knot undone. This knot has no such shortcoming. One tug and it falls away.

Tying

Given a loop of some kind (an angler's knot is illustrated), wrap and tuck as shown (*figures 1–3*). Tighten the knot.

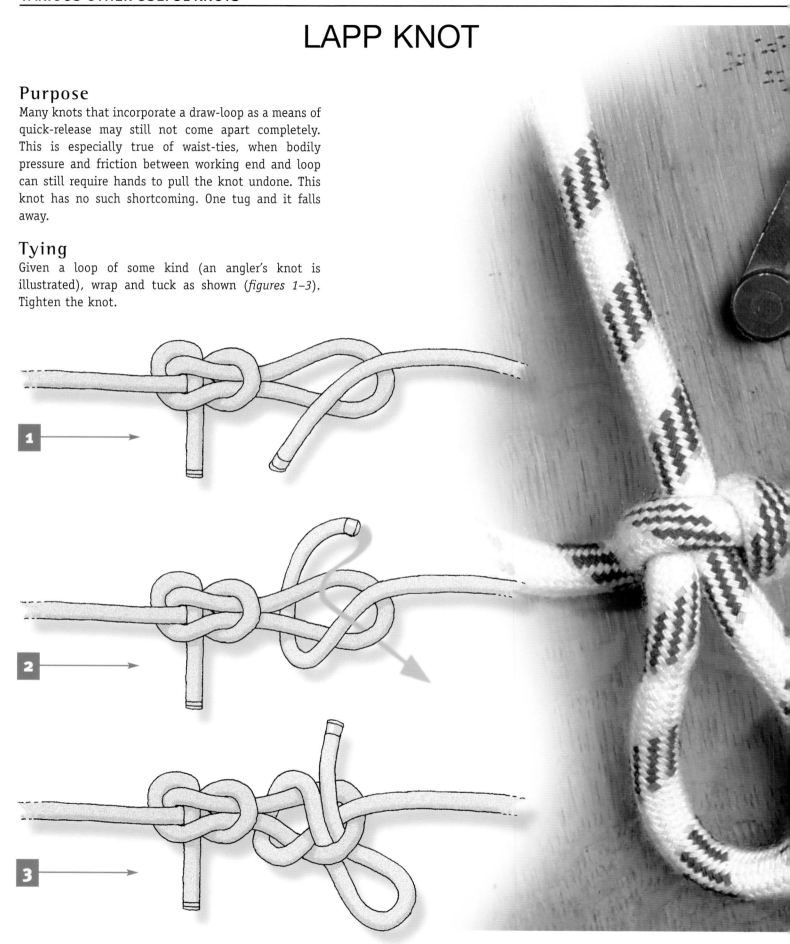

1

2

3

Knot lore

This almost unknown knot has been around for at least one hundred years, although it is often dismissed somewhat contemptuously as a false sheet bend. Several contemporary knot tyers—all members of the International Guild of Knot Tyers—have separately come forward in support of it. They include Pieter van de Griend (Faroe Islands), Charles Warner (Australia) and Robert Pont (France) who in *Knotting Matters* (April 1996) told of its use in Lapland in knife lanyards as well as for hitching reindeers to sleds.

CARRICK BEND

Purpose

Traditionally this bend was recommended for cables and large hawsers and—perhaps as a consequence of its being used in this way—it has an undeserved reputation for being a strong knot, when it actually reduces the breaking strength of lines by up to 30% or more. It is, nevertheless, a useful bend and just as well suited to smaller cordage.

Tying

Create a loop in one line and interweave the working end of the other line as shown (*figures 1–2*). Make sure that the short ends emerge on opposite sides of the knot, since there is a belief that it is more secure like that. When pulled tight, the knot capsizes into another form entirely, and it is this final arrangement that it is useful (*figure 3*).

Knot lore

Some knot tyers know this as the true or double carrick bend, since there are other lesser versions. This one was featured in *Seamanship for the Merchant Service* (1922) by Felix Reisenberg, but named even earlier in *Vocabulaire des Termes de Marine* (1783) by M. Lescallier. As a heraldic device, with both ends on the same side of the knot, it is older still. A number of them in plaster are used as decorative devices in the Elizabethan plasterwork of Ormonde Castle at Carrick-on-Suir in Ireland, and it was the badge of the English leader Hereward the Wake who, from his stronghold on the Isle of Ely, revolted against William the Conqueror in 1070.

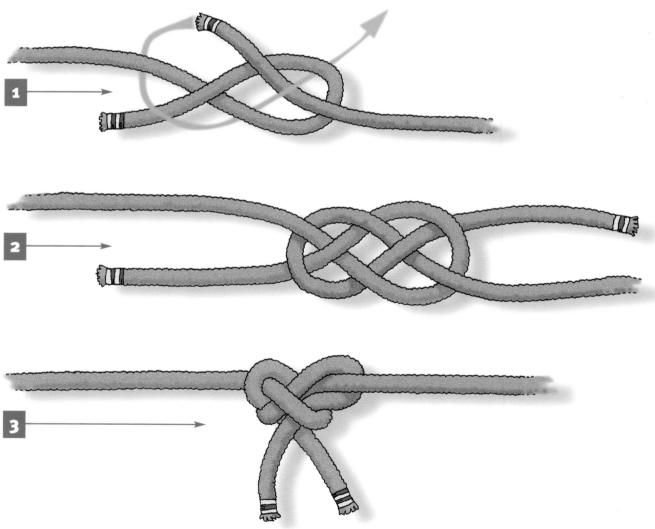

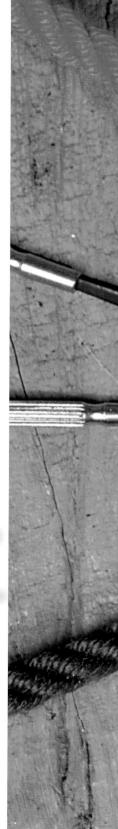

TURK'S HEAD (3 lead x 4 bight)

Purpose

This is a practical and ornamental binding knot.

Tying #1

To make it flat, tie a modified carrick bend (*previous page*), with both ends emerging on the same side of the knot (*figures 1–2*). Tuck the working end alongside the standing part (*figure 3*). The knot that has been created has two distinct features—three plaited parts (known as leads) and four rim-parts (called bights)—which distinguish it from any other Turk's heads. These are abbreviated to 3L x 4B. Follow the original lead around—going over where it goes over, under where it goes under—until the knot has been doubled (*figure 4*) or tripled.

Tying #2

While the 3L x 4B Turk's head tied above may be slipped over the end of a finger, or other foundation, and so turned into a plaited ring or bracelet, it is better to tie it directly. Wrap and turn and weave as shown (*figures 5–8*). Double and triple the lead to complete the knot (*figure 9*). In a three-ply knot, by inserting a second cord (of a contrasting hue), an even more decorative appearance can be achieved. Pull it tight patiently, a bit at a time, working from one end of the cord to the other several times.

Knot lore

The 3L x 4B Turk's head in its flattened form is the motif of the International Guild of Knot Tyers, adopted in 1982 and still in use, to indicate their commitment to both practical and ornamental knotting. As a bracelet, it is the curiously named "woggle" traditionally worn by Boy Scouts to hold their neck scarves in place.

The Turk's head knot has been used since time immemorial. Entire manuals have been written about just this one family of knots. Some knot tyers do nothing else. Enormous Turk's heads have been completed, by scaling up the number of leads and bights, and their ultimate size is limited only by the available length of line (and patience). Then, as a change from the regular over-under-over sequence, herringbone or twill weaves (over 2-under 2) and other variations are possible. Rim bights may be made to leap-frog one another in complicated picot patterns. T-shaped and cruciform Turk's heads are possible. Using certain formulas, graph paper and a special kind of slide rule designed for the purpose, candelabras and hollow spheres have been created. The ramifications of the Turk's head knot are truly infinite.

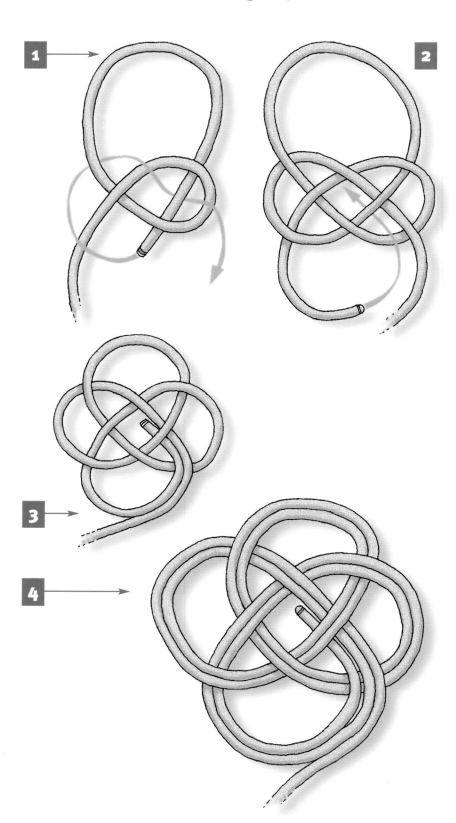

KNIFE LANYARD KNOT

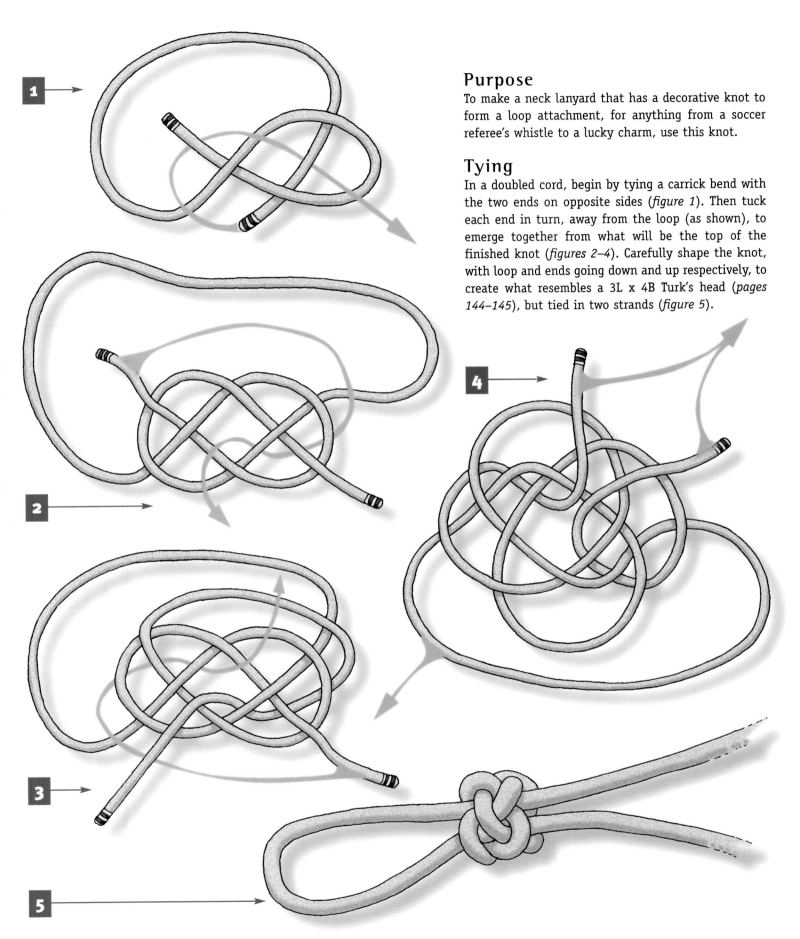

Purpose

To make a neck lanyard that has a decorative knot to form a loop attachment, for anything from a soccer referee's whistle to a lucky charm, use this knot.

Tying

In a doubled cord, begin by tying a carrick bend with the two ends on opposite sides (*figure 1*). Then tuck each end in turn, away from the loop (as shown), to emerge together from what will be the top of the finished knot (*figures 2–4*). Carefully shape the knot, with loop and ends going down and up respectively, to create what resembles a 3L x 4B Turk's head (*pages 144–145*), but tied in two strands (*figure 5*).

RING HITCH

Purpose

Attach any lanyard or neck cord to whatever it suspends, from a jack-knife to a sports coach's stopwatch, by means of this simplest of hitches.

Tying

Either the loop or bight must be long enough to pass right over the object to be attached (as illustrated) or it must be possible to thread the other end of the lanyard through itself. In this instance lift the object through as shown (*figure 1*). Pull tight (*figure 2*).

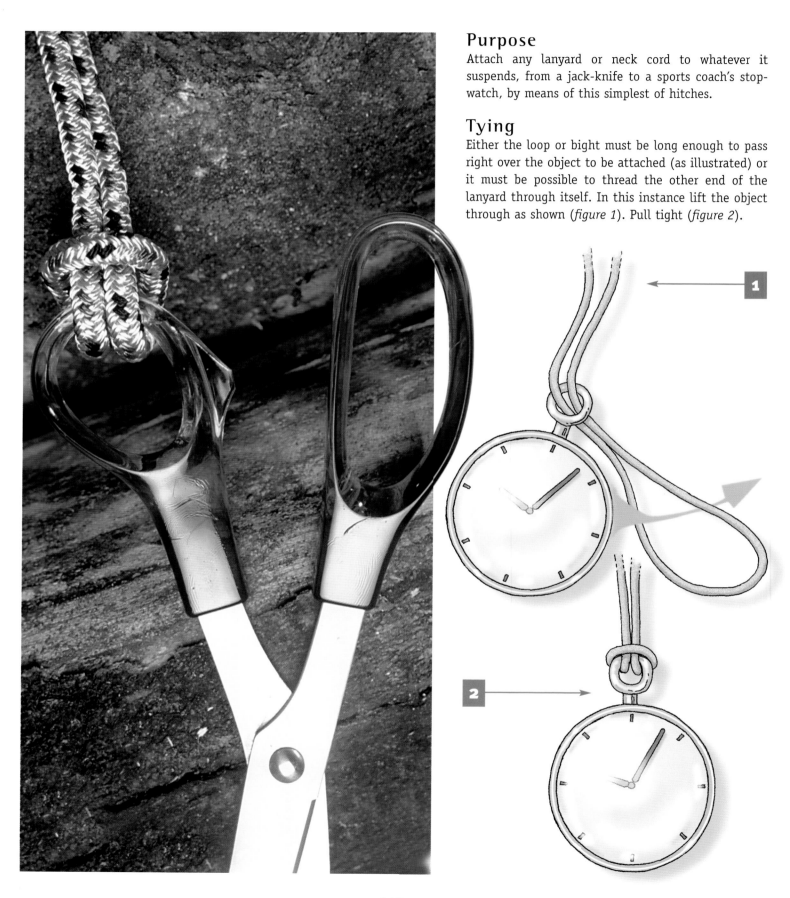

TURK'S HEAD (3 lead x 5 bight)

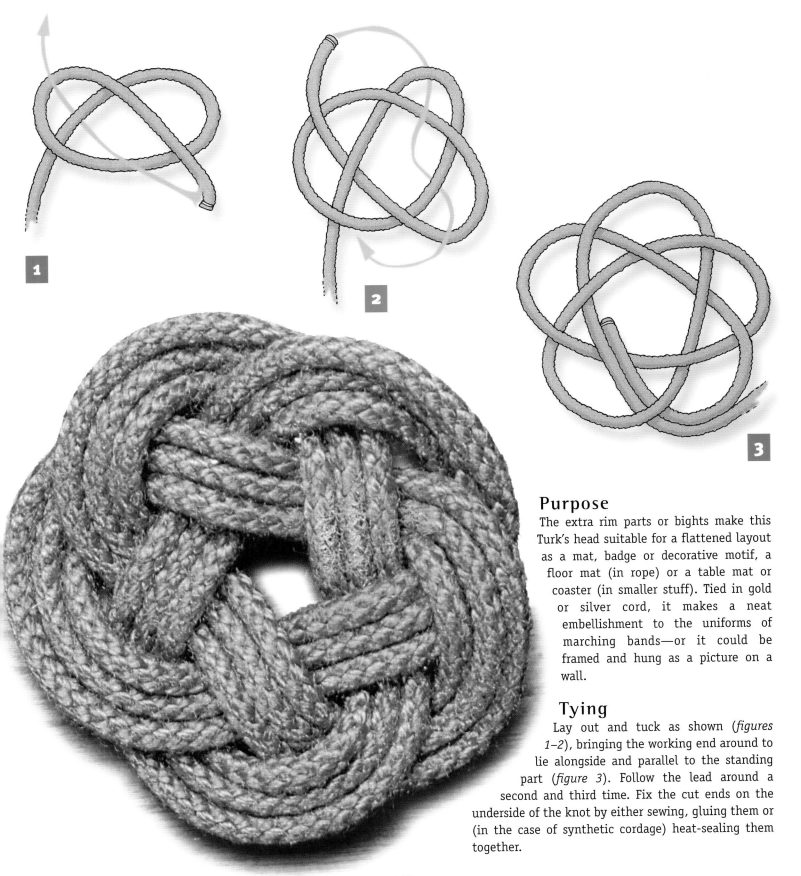

Purpose

The extra rim parts or bights make this Turk's head suitable for a flattened layout as a mat, badge or decorative motif, a floor mat (in rope) or a table mat or coaster (in smaller stuff). Tied in gold or silver cord, it makes a neat embellishment to the uniforms of marching bands—or it could be framed and hung as a picture on a wall.

Tying

Lay out and tuck as shown (*figures 1–2*), bringing the working end around to lie alongside and parallel to the standing part (*figure 3*). Follow the lead around a second and third time. Fix the cut ends on the underside of the knot by either sewing, gluing them or (in the case of synthetic cordage) heat-sealing them together.

149

TURK'S HEAD (5 lead x 4 bight)

Purpose

This is a slightly bigger and more elaborate knot—but still a square Turk's head, that is one in which the number of leads and bights only differs by one. It makes a handsome, secure whipping for a rope's end, or a decorative collar over any other foundation for which the basic 3L x 4B knot is too skimpy.

Tying

Wrap, tuck and weave as shown (*figures 1–5*), bringing the working end back alongside the standing part. Follow the original lead around as many times as necessary to fill in the spaces within the open texture of the initial knot (*figure 6*).

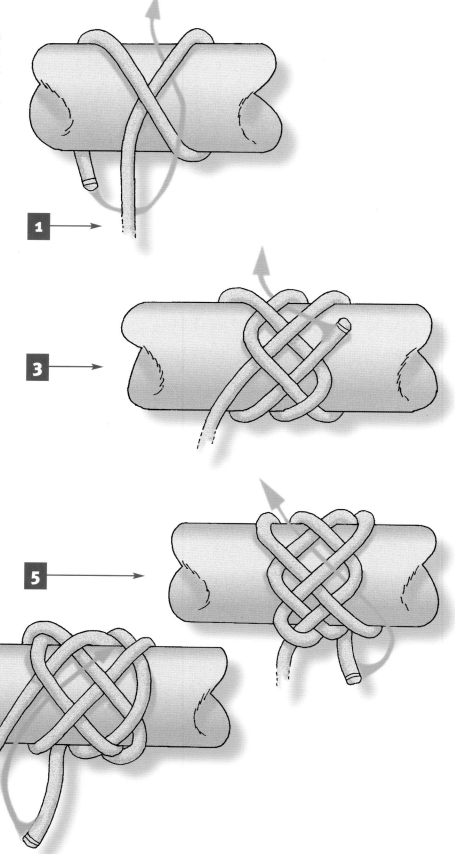

TURK'S HEAD (T-SHAPED)

Purpose

Although there are practical purposes for this knot—to cover the junctions of handrails and their uprights, or to mark (for recognition in the dark) the midships spoke of a yacht's wheel—this is another of those challenging knots that it is satisfying to tie merely for the sake of doing it.

Tying

Work methodically, checking every illustrated step before moving on to the next. Arrange each stage as shown and hold it in place—do not allow it to distort—as each succeeding tuck is made. Note how it is frequently necessary to turn the work over, so as to make tucks on the reverse side of the knot. The steps where one is most likely to go astray and become lost are the early ones (*figures 1–8*). When done faultlessly, however, two regular ladders appear through which a pair of locking tucks are inserted (*figures 8–9* and *11–12*). Double or triple the original lead to create a two-ply or three-ply knot and tighten gradually, a bit at a time (*figure 13*).

Knot lore

This is essentially a 5B x 6L Turk's head, modified by the creation of a hole to accommodate the right-angled entry of the spoke to the foundation. It was devised by David Fukuhara (a member of the International Guild of Knot Tyers) of Vancouver, Canada, and published in *Knotting Matters* (February 1999).

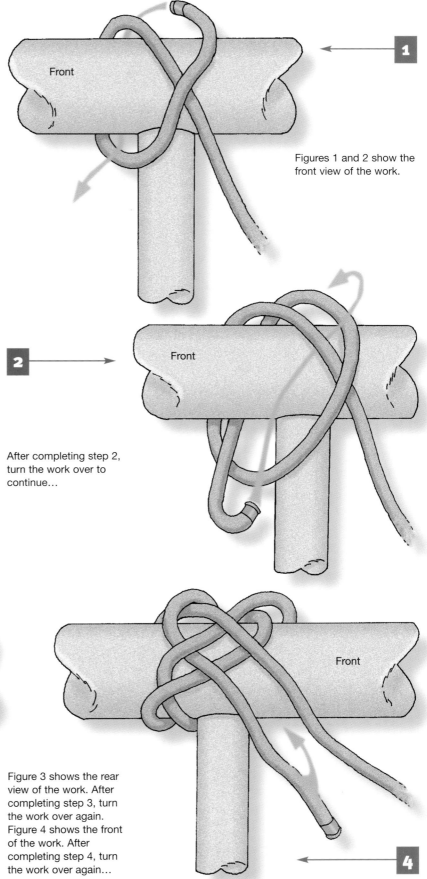

Figures 1 and 2 show the front view of the work.

After completing step 2, turn the work over to continue…

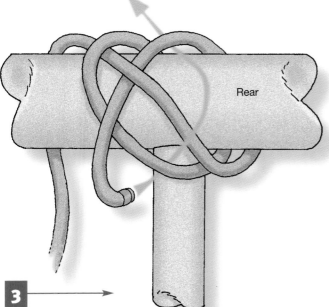

Figure 3 shows the rear view of the work. After completing step 3, turn the work over again. Figure 4 shows the front of the work. After completing step 4, turn the work over again…

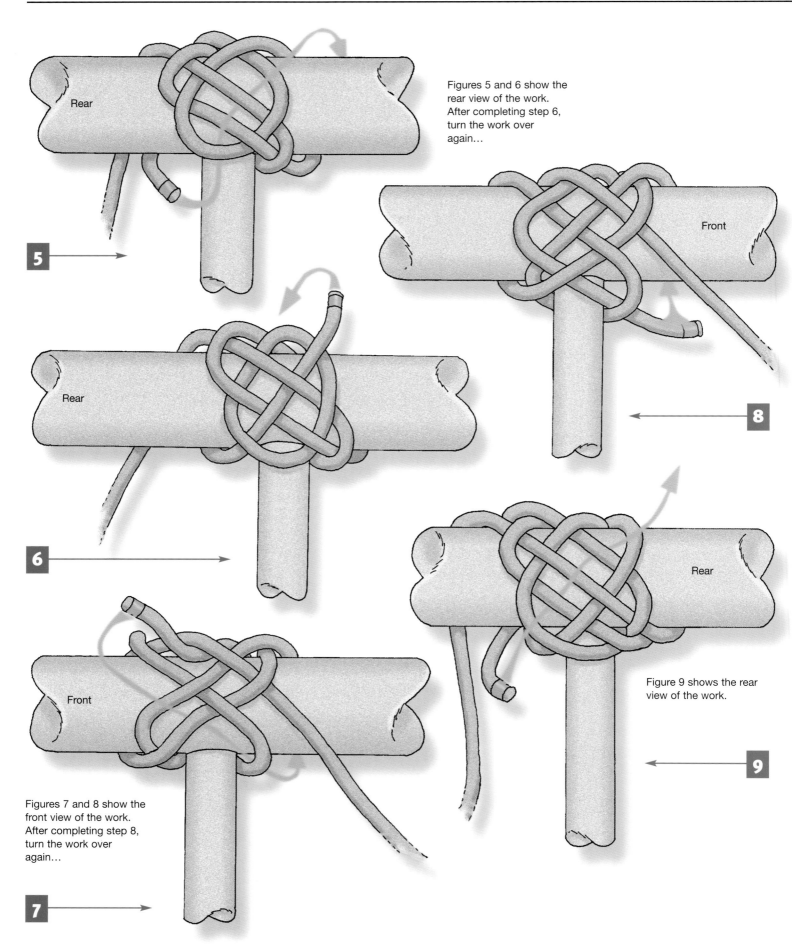

5

Figures 5 and 6 show the rear view of the work. After completing step 6, turn the work over again…

6

8

7

Figures 7 and 8 show the front view of the work. After completing step 8, turn the work over again…

9

Figure 9 shows the rear view of the work.

154

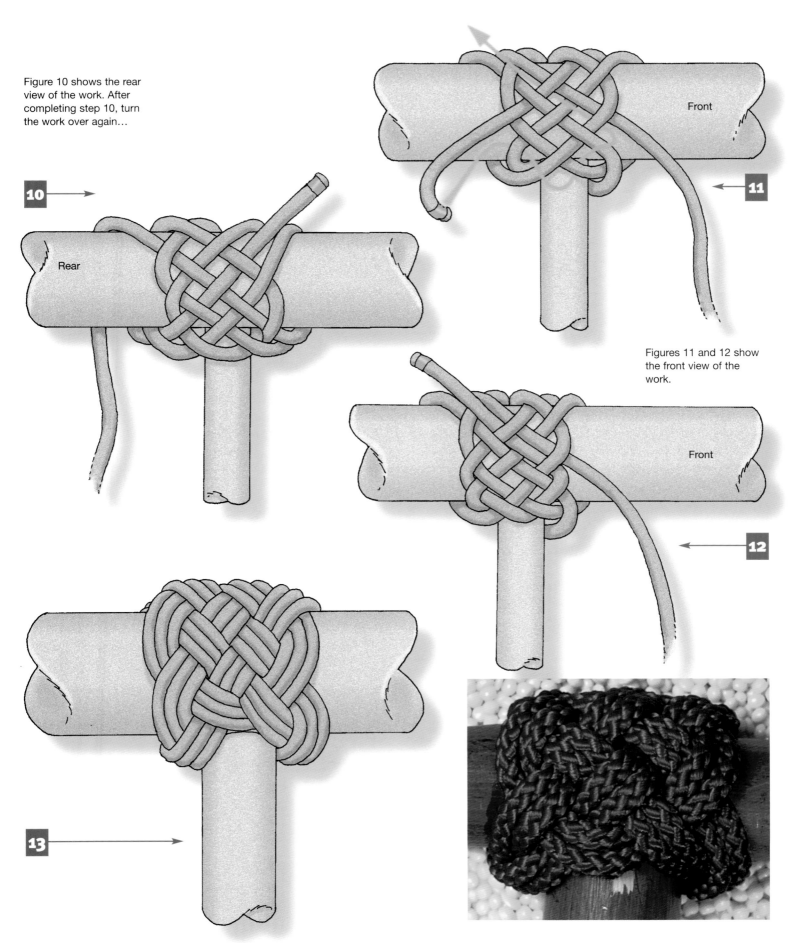

Figure 10 shows the rear view of the work. After completing step 10, turn the work over again...

Front

Rear

10 →

11 ←

Figures 11 and 12 show the front view of the work.

Front

12 ←

13 →

SUMMARY

And many knots unravel'd by the Road;
But not the Master Knot of Human Fate.

(Quatro XXXIV of the *Rubáiyát of Omar Khayyám*,
Persian astronomer & poet, c.1050–1123)

Two thirds of the knots, bends and hitches featured in this book are classics (from the bowline and clove hitch to the Matthew Walker and the sheet bend), their names well-known even to those who cannot tie them. Some, like the overhand knot and simple noose, are no doubt ancient in origin. All would be instantly recognizable to any Elizabethan or Georgian individual who had worked with cordage.

The other third portrays less well known specimens (such as the Lapp knot), together with some twentieth century innovations (Ashley's stopper knot and the boom hitch), and even a few virtually new discoveries (among them the double figure of eight hitch, the snuggle hitch and the vice versa). A few, like the Chinese lanyard knot and the T-shaped Turk's head are intended to test the minds and tease the fingers of the ablest knotting practitioners. All who have successfully come to grips with half of the specimens in this book can rate themselves knottologists of more than average ability. Well done, indeed.

What next? For those who merely require to know a handful of the right knots for their employment or leisure pursuits, the contents of this book are more than adequate. Its purchase price will be amply repaid by learning and putting into practice a fraction of the knots, bends or hitches described and illustrated within it. Others, in whom a previously unsuspected and dormant fascination for the lure and lore of knotting has been aroused, will now be turned on to learn more. For them other knotting publications await discovery. Two merit special mention.

The Ashley Book of Knots by Clifford Warren Ashley, originally published in the U.S.A. in 1944, is the ultimate and indispensable guide for all dedicated knot tyers. Nobody can talk for long about knots without mentioning it. Not only is it the seminal source of knotting know-how, it is also delightful background browsing, since its 620 pages and 4,000 knot drawings are enlivened by scores of amusing sketches, for the author was an accomplished marine artist and professional illustrator. It is unarguably the best knot book in the world and, despite a generally high price, great value-for-money.

The *Encyclopedia of Knots & Fancy Work* by Frenchman Raoul Graumont and American John Hensel pre-dates Ashley by five years. Illustrated throughout with monochrome photographs—remarkable when first published, but badly dated—and with a tricky maze of an index, it does not inspire the same affection as Ashley (even in those who use it a lot). Nevertheless, it too is magnificent, with 690 pages including 347 full-page photographic

plates, and it is the other major source of vintage knot-work.

The next step for anyone—novice or expert—eager to learn more knotting must be to consider meeting other knot tyers. To do so, contact the International Guild of Knot Tyers.

The International Guild of Knot Tyers

The Guild was established in 1982 by 27 individuals and now has a membership exceeding 1,000 in territories from Alaska to Zimbabwe. It is a UK registered education charity and anyone interested in knots may join.

Guild members are brought together by their common pursuit of knot tying. In Britain two major weekend meetings are held each year, with talks, demonstrations and expert tuition freely available, where cordage, rope-working tools and books are also bought, sold or swapped. In countries and regions where many Guild members are clustered together, local branches have formed and these arrange more frequent gatherings and activities.

The worldwide membership keeps in touch via a handbook of members' names, addresses and other contact details, as well as the quarterly magazine *Knotting Matters*, which is full of informed articles, expert tips, letters, editorial comment, news and views about everything imaginable on the knot-tying scene.

For USA details, see page 158, and for application and international membership subscription fees, contact:

Nigel Harding (IGKT Honorary Secretary)
16, Egles Grove
Uckfield
East Sussex TN22 2BY
England
Tel: +44 (0)1825 760425
email: *igkt@nigelharding.demon.co.uk*

Knotting may also be found on the Internet.

GLOSSARY OF TERMS

BEND Generic name for those knots that bind (or bend) two separate ropes together.

BIGHT Any slack section of a line when it forms a partial loop.

BREAKING STRENGTH A manufacturer's calculation or estimate, expressed in kilograms or tonnes, of the load a rope will sustain before failing. It takes no account of factors (such as wear and tear, knots) that may drastically reduce this figure. (See also Safe Working Load).

CABLE Three right-handed hawser-laid ropes laid up left-handed into a nine-strand rope; or, more generally, any large rope.

CORD Smaller cordage under $^3/_8$ in (10 mm) diameter

CORE Yarns laid or braided to create a heart within braided cordage that is either inert or contributes a degree of strength, elasticity or some other quality to the line

DACRON (See Terylene)

DOG To contrive a temporary running eye in the working end of a line by wrapping the working end around its own standing part.

EFFICIENCY A very approximate estimation of a knot's strength, expressed as a percentage of the theoretical breaking strength of the unknotted rope in which it is tied.

ELBOW Two acute crossing points created in a loop or between any two knot parts.

EYE A small round loop.

FIBER The smallest element in all cordage of vegetable origin.

FILAMENT The smallest element in all cordage of synthetic origin (See both Monofilament and Multifilament)

FRAY The unintentional or deliberate unlaying of a rope's end to its component strands, yarns and filaments.

HARD LAID Any cordage rendered stiff and less flexible due to the tension imparted during manufacture.

HAWSER Traditional rope, usually of three strands and laid right-handed.

HEART (See *Core*)

HITCH Generic name for those knots that attach a line or lanyard securely to a fixed ring, rail, spar, post or other firm anchorage point.

KERNMANTEL (Literally core-sheath) The European name for some climbing ropes.

KNOT Generic term for any cordage entanglement—accidental or deliberate—that is not a bend or a hitch.

LANYARD A short length of cord used to lash, secure or suspend an item.

LAY The direction in which rope strands spiral as they recede from the person tying the knot, either right-handed (clockwise) or left-handed (counter-clockwise).

LEAD (Pronounced "leed") The direction taken by the working end as it goes around or through an object or a knot.

LINE Any rope with a specific use (tow-line, guy-line, washing line).

LOCKING TUCK The final tuck, usually with a regular over-under sequence, without which a knot layout is incomplete and insecure.

LOOP A bight with a crossing point.

MONOFILAMENT A continuous extruded synthetic filament of uniform diameter and circular cross-section less than 50 microns (one micron = 0.000001m).

MULTIFILAMENT A cluster of very fine continuously extruded synthetic filaments of uniform diameter and circular cross-section that are less than 50 microns (one micron = 0.000001m).

NATURAL FIBER Cordage material of vegetable origin.

NIP The point within a knot where friction is concentrated.

NOOSE A free-running, sliding or adjustable loop.

NYLON An artificial material used in the manufacture of cordage and characterized by its elasticity.

POLYESTER (See Terylene)

POLYETHYLENE An artificial material used in the manufacture of cheap, hard-wearing and lightweight cordage.

POLYPROPYLENE A versatile artificial material used for a variety of modern cordage.

ROPE Strictly speaking, cordage over $^3/_8$ in (10 mm) in diameter.

S-LAID Left-handed cordage.

SAFE WORKING LOAD The estimated load—often as little as one fifth (or less) of the actual breaking strength—a rope may be certified to withstand, taking into account various weakening factors. (See also Breaking Strength)

SECURITY The essential stability of any

knot when subjected to a variable or intermittent load.

SMALL STUFF An informal and imprecise term for any cordage thinner than a rope.

SOFT LAID Any cordage rendered more flexible by reduced tension during manufacture.

SPLIT FILM Artificial ribbon-like filaments produced from a plastic sheet.

STANDING END The inactive end of cord. (See also Working End)

STANDING PART That part of a rope or cord anywhere between the working end and the standing end.

STAPLE FIBERS Graded vegetable fibers of limited length and strength; also discontinuous artificial fibers created by chopping extruded synthetic filaments into shorter lengths.

STRAND The largest element of a rope, made from contra-twisted yarns.

STRENGTH The integral ability of a knot to withstand a load.

STRING Relatively cheap and disposable small cord and twine of domestic quality.

SYNTHETIC CORDAGE Rope and smaller cordage products that are made from artificial (manmade) filaments, staple fibers or split film.

TERYLENE An artificial material characterized by its lack of elasticity and resistance to wear from abrasion.

THREAD Fine line.

WHIPPING A generic term for various bindings used to prevent a rope's end from fraying.

WORKING END The active end of a rope or cord. (See also Standing End)

YARN The basic element of rope strands, spun from natural or synthetic fibers.

Z-LAID Right-handed cordage.

SUPPLIERS OF CORDAGE

In addition to the general advice given in the introduction to this book concerning where cordage of all kinds might be found and bought, a number of suppliers exist from whom specialized products and technical advice can be obtained. Wholesalers have minimum order requirements but can generally provide details of retail outlets able to sell lesser quantities. Detailed lists and prices are available on request.

NORTH AMERICA

The Knot Shoppe—and Alaska Museum of Fancy Knots (Daniel Callahan)
c/o Arctic Resource Center,
2211 Arca Drive, Anchorage, AK 99508
Tel: 907 277 6677 ext 211
email: *knot_tyer@hotmail.com*

Alaska Fancy Knot Tyers Club
(Dan Callahan)
http://clubs.snap.com/knots2/index.html

IGKT—North American Branch
Secretary: John Burke, 4417 Academy, Dearborn Heights, MI 48125-2205
Tel: 313 562 4393

IGKT—Pacific Americas Branch
Contacts: Joe Schmidbauer, 1805 Kingsford Drive, Corona, CA 91720
Tel: 909 737 4948
email: *koolkatz@prodigy.net*, or
Lindsey Philpott, 3646 Gaviota Avenue, Long Beach, CA 90807-4306
Tel: 562 595 8854
email: linseyph@aol.com

EUROPE

English Braids (Marine Sales Manager: David Ierston)
Spring Lane, Malvern, Worcestershire WR14 1AL, England
Tel: +44 (0)1684 892 222
Fax: +44 (0)684 892 111
The marine sales division of this major

international manufacturer caters for the recreational sector and sail boat racing. Suppliers of barrier ropes, starter cords, shock cords, whipping twines, webbing and web-lash securing systems.

Eurorope Limited
4 Phoenix Court, Atkinson Way, Foxhills Industrial Estate, Scunthorpe DN15 8QJ, England
Tel: +44 (0)1724 280 480
Fax: +44 (0)1724 857 750
Suppliers of rope, cord, twines, nets, lifting gear slings and accessories.

Footrope Knots (Des & Liz Pawson, members of the International Guild of Knot Tyers)
501 Wherstead Road, Ipswich, Suffolk IP2 8LL, England
Tel: +44 (0)1473 690 090
Suppliers of traditional ropes, cordage and smaller stuff; wire rope and chain; canvas; rope work and rigging tools;

fittings; fenders; knotboards; chest beckets, bell-ropes and other knot work; books (new, secondhand and rare). Personal service and expert advice available to all customers. Their unique rope work museum may be visited free of charge (by prior arrangement).

Jimmy Green Marine
New Cut (off Fore Street), Beer, East Devon Heritage Coast, EX12 3JH, England
Tel: +44 (0)1297 20744
Fax: +44 (0)1297 20788
Suppliers of a range of boat ropes and riggings; bannister ropes; shock cords; guard-rail and stowage netting; rope ladders; webbing; and every kind of nautical accessory.

K.J.K. Ropeworks (Kevin Keatley is a member of the International Guild of Knot Tyers)
Town Living Farmhouse, Puddington, Tiverton, Devon EX16 8LW, England
Tel/fax: +44 (0)1884 860 692

Supplier of cords and fittings, especially colored synthetic braids ideal for knot tying.

Leanda
39 Borrowdale Drive, Norwich, Norfolk NR1 4LY, England
Tel/fax: +44 (0)1603 434 707
Textile craft equipment manufacturers; specialists in Japanese-style braiding and passementerie equipment; accessories for spinning and weaving; also a book list.

Marlow Ropes Limited
(Market Coordinator: James Martin)
Diplocks Way, Hailsham, East Sussex BN27 3JS, England
Tel: +44 (0)1323 847 234
Fax: +44 (0)1323 440 093
email: yachting@marlowropes.com
Website: http://www.marlowropes.com
Major manufacturer and international market leader in yacht rope technology and such accessories as shock-cord,

barrier ropes, toe-strap and buoyancy bag webbing, whipping twine, splicing kits, sail repair tapes.

Ann Norman (a member of the International Guild of Knot Tyers)
Sagaman, Aston Road, Bampton, Oxfordshire OX18 2AL, England
Tel/fax: +44 (0)1993 850 823
email: sagaman@compuserve.com
Designer, handweaver and maker of cords, including four-strand cords, and ropes of traditional laid structure. Advice offered and commissions accepted.

Oakhurst Quality Products Limited
(Brenda Risdon)
Warsop Trading Estate, Hever Road, Edenbridge, Kent TN8 5LD, England
Tel: +44 (0)1732 866 668
Fax: +44 (0)1732 864 555
Wholesale suppliers of rope, twine, cordage, chain, doormats, work gloves, garden sundries.

INDEX

A New System of Knotting; 20, 125, 139
A Treatise on Rigging; 108;
Abraham, R.M.; 9
activities and knots; 6
Allgemeines Wörterbuch der Marine; 75, 126
Allied Chemicals; 11
alpine butterfly knot; 18, **109**
American cowboys; 9
ancient cultures and knots; 7
angler's knot; 139
angler's loop; 26–27
animal origin fibers in rope; 10
Asher's bottle sling; 124–125
Asher, Dr. Harry; 20, 125, 139
Ashley's stopper knot; 18, **29**, 47
Ashley, Clifford Warren; 17, 29, 56, 63, 98, 104, 156
astronauts and knots; 6
Baffin island; 78
bag, sack or miller's knot; 31
bend, description; 17
Berners (Barnes), Dame Juliana; 7, 44

bight; 18
binding knot; 6
binding knot, description; 17
Boas, Franz; 78
Bois Brule tribe; 120
Book of Knots; 56
boom hitch; 104
bowline; 6
bowline in the bight; 75
braid knot; 128–129
braid-on-braid ropes; 13
braided lines; 13
breaking strength of ropes; 18
British warfare and knots; 8
Brown, Ronnie; 6
bull hitch; 120–121
buntline hitch; 88–89
Calico Printers Association; 10
care of cordage; 16
carrick bend; 142–143
cat's cradles; 8
Cennini, Cennio; 8

Chen, Lydia; 137
chinese cloverleaf; 132–133
chinese lanyard knot; 136–137
Chisnall, Robert; 66, 76
clove hitch; 6, 17, **86–87**
coiling cordage; 16
color of ropes; 15
common bowline; 70–71
common whipping; 106–107
constrictor knot; 15, **94–95**
Cooper, James Fenimore; 69
cordage construction; 12
cordage materials; 10
cost of ropes; 15
cotton, use in ropes; 10
crossing point; 18
DNA and knots; 6
double bowline; 74
double constrictor knot; 96–97
double figure of eight hitch; 102–103
double fisherman's knot; 51
double overhand knot; 47

INDEX

double overhand loop; **52**
double overhand noose; **50**
double reef bow; 18
double sheet bend; 82
draw-loop; 18
Du Pont laboratories; 10–11
Dyneema™, use in ropes; 11
Egyptians and knots; 6
eight-strand cable; 12
Elements and Practice of Rigging and Seamanship; 45, 80, 108
ends of rope; 15
Eskimo bowline; 17, 78–79
Falconer, William; 86
figure eight becket hitch; 59
figure of eight bend; 62–63
figure of eight coil; 68
figure of eight hitch; 57
figure of eight knot; 17, 54–55
figure of eight loop; 58
figure of eight noose; 56
figure of eight triple loop; 66–67
figure of eight twin loops; 64–65
fisherman's bend; 46
fisherman's knot; 18, 35
flax, use in ropes; 10
Flemish bend; 60
Flemish loop; 58
granny knot; 40
Graumont, Raoul; 156
ground line hitch coil; 99
Hansen, David H.; 9
hard-laid ropes; 13
hawser-laid core braid construction; 13
hawser-laid rope construction; 12
heat-sealing cut synthetic rope; 15
Hensel, John; 6
Herbert, Sir Alan; 70
highwayman's hitch; 18, 114–115
hitch, description; 17
hunter's or rigger's bend; 36–37
Hunter, Dr. Edward; 36
I.G. Farbenindistrie; 10
Imperial Chemical Industries; 10
International Guild of Knot Tyers; 18, 20, 36, 53, 66, 84, 100, 102, 116, 120, 144, **156**
Italian hemp; 10
jug, jar or bottle sling; 126–127
jute, use in ropes; 10
kernmantel; 13
Kevlar™, use in ropes; 11
killick hitch; 108
knife lanyard knot; 146; 147
knot efficiency; 18
knot finder; 22
knot names; 18
knot security; 20
knot strength; 18
knot terms, description; 18
Knots and Fancy Work; 156
knots in British warfare; 8
knots in DNA; 6
knots in land surveying; 7
knots in Roman engineering; 7
Knotting Matters; 116, 120

knotting repertoire; 17
knotting terms; 17
land surveying and knots; 7
Lapp knot; 140–141
law of loop, hitch & bight; 20
left-handed rope; 12
Lescallier, M.; 142
Lever, Darcy; 75
Little, E.W.; 126
Log Book Notes; 126
loop/noose, description; 17–18
Los Angeles, airship; 38
Lovins, Amory Bloch; 36
magnus hitch; 91
Mandeville, Desmond; 18
Markham, Gervase; 7
Matthew Walker knot; 134–135
McLeay, Heather; 105
melting points of synthetic ropes; 11
midshipman's hitch; 92–93
monofilaments; 12
multifilaments; 12
natural fiber cordage; 10
nip; 18
Nobbs, Robert; 7
Nuttal, Owen K,; 100, 102
nylon, use in ropes; 10
one-way sheet bend; 83
overhand knot with draw-loop; 25
overhand loop; 30
oysterman's stopper knot; 29
Padgett, Alan; 41
parallel core braid construction; 13
PBO, use in ropes; 11
pedigree cow hitch; 118–119
Persall-Smith, Logan; 9
pile, post or stake hitch; 116–117
plafond knot; 137
plaited core braid construction; 13
plaited ropes; 12
Plato's Laws; 8
Polyester, use in ropes; 10
polyethylene, use in ropes; 10
Polymide, use in ropes; 10
polypropylene, use in ropes; 11
Port of Lisbon, 16th century; 9
preventing fraying; 24
Prusik, Karl; 122
prusik knot; 122–123
Queen Cleopatra; 7
reef (or square) knot; 40
reef (or square) knot loop; 110–111
reef knot; 17–18
Reisenberg, Felix; 142
right-handed rope; 12
ring hitch; 148
Röding, Johann; 126
rolling hitch; 90–91
Roman shipping; 8
Romans and knots; 7
Roosevelt, Franklin D.; 53
ropemaking; 12
Rosendahl, Charles; 38

Rosenow, Frank; 84
Ross, Sir John; 78
round turn & two half-hitches; 17, 45
rustler's knot; 18, 130
Ryan, Donald P.; 9
S-laid rope; 12
safety with looped ropes; 64
Scout Pioneering; 109
Seamanship for the Merchant; 142
securing ends of cut rope; 15
sheet bend; 6, 17, 80–81
simple noose; 28
simple overhand knot; 18, 24
sliding figure of eight bend; 60–61
Smith, Bruce; 41
Smith, Phil D.; 36
snuggle hitch; 100–101
Spectra™, use in ropes; 11
square knot; 18, 130–131
standing end; 18
standing part; 18
Steel, David; 80, 108
Stevenson, Robert Louis; 85
stopper knot, description; 17
strangle knot; 48–49
strangle knot coil; 48–49
stringing musical instruments; 24
Sweet, John; 109
synthetic fiber cordage; 10
Tait, Peter Guthrie; 6
The Alternative Knot Book; 20, 138
The Ashley Book of Knots; 156
The Compleat Angler; 44
the frustrator; 112–113
three-layered core braid construction; 13
three-way sheet bend; 84
timber hitch; 17, 108
transom knot; 98
Treatyse of Fyshinge with an Angle; 44
tricorn loop; 32–33
triple bowline; 76–77
turk's head (3L x 4B); 144–145
turk's head (3L x 5B); 149
turk's head (5L x 4B); 150–151
turk's head (T-shaped); 152–155
twin bowline bend; 72
Universal Dictionary of the Marine; 86
Vectran™, use in ropes; 11
vegetable fiber cordage; 10
Venables, Robert; 7
Venetian shipping; 8
vice versa; 17, 18, 138–139
Vocabulaire des Termes de Marine; 142
Walton, Izaak; 7, 26, 44
water bowline; 73
water or tape knot; 44
West Country whipping; 42–43
Wilde, Oscar; 15
woggle; 144
working end; 18
wrapped and reef-knotted coil; 41
Young Officer's Sheet Anchor; 75
Z-laid rope; 12
zeppelin bend (or Rosendahl's knot); 38–39